The Discover Your *True North* Fieldbook

The Discover Your *True North* Fieldbook

A Personal Guide to Finding Your Authentic Leadership

Second Edition

Nick Craig

Bill George

Scott Snook

WILEY

Published by John Wiley & Sons, Inc., Hoboken, New Jersey.
Published simultaneously in Canada.

For general information on our other products and services or for technical support, please contact our Customer Care Department within the United States at (800) 762–2974, outside the United States at (317) 572–3993 or fax (317) 572–4002.

Wiley publishes in a variety of print and electronic formats and by print-on-demand. Some material included with standard print versions of this book may not be included in e-books or in print-on-demand. If this book refers to media such as a CD or DVD that is not included in the version you purchased, you may download this material at http://booksupport.wiley.com. For more information about Wiley products, visit www.wiley.com.

Library of Congress Cataloging-in-Publication Data:
George, Bill (William W.)
  The discover your true north fieldbook: a personal guide to finding your authentic
leadership / Nick Craig, Bill George, Scott Snook.—Revised and updated.
    pages cm
  Includes index.
   ISBN 978–1–119–10355–4 (pbk.); ISBN 978–1–119–10356–1 (ePDF);
ISBN 978–1–119–10357–8 (ePub)
  1. Leadership. 2. Organizational effectiveness.   I. Craig, Nick, 1960-
II. Snook, Scott A., 1958-   III. Title.
   HD57.7.G458143 2015
   658.4'092—dc23
                                                        2015013777

Printed in the United States of America

10 9 8 7 6 5 4 3 2 1

Bill George dedicates this book to his colleagues Nick Craig and Scott Snook,
who have devoted their lives to enabling leaders
to discover their True North.

Nick Craig dedicates this book to the authentic leaders in his life,
who showed him the way by being just themselves.

Scott Snook dedicates this book to his wife Kathi, and their five children,
Sean, Kyle, Megan, Robby, and Jessica.

Contents

Preface
Why an Updated *Fieldbook*?

Since writing the original version of this fieldbook, we have had the privilege of working with over 10,000 individuals on their journey to becoming more authentic leaders. Our experience has ranged from teaching the Authentic Leadership Development MBA course at Harvard Business School to running custom True North programs with senior executives with global responsibilities.

In the process, we have learned a great deal about how people discover and implement their True North. Having worked with many of these individuals over an extended period of time, we have come to understand their long-term journey and what it takes to stay the course.

As Bill said in the Preface of the first edition:

"Leadership matters. It matters a great deal—to our organizations and institutions, to the people who work in them, and to the people who are served by them. For our society to function effectively, we need authentic leaders who can encourage people to perform at their best and step up and lead themselves."

"I wrote True North because I have a passion to see more people in all walks of life lead authentically and because I wanted to help people like you discover your authentic leadership."

In conjunction with *Discover Your True North*, we have amassed our insights and learning to create a significantly updated guide to assist you on your journey to authentic leadership. As you navigate the uncharted territory of the twenty-first century, we hope our fieldbook assists you in becoming a highly effective—and authentic—leader, one who follows your True North and stays the course!

WHY THIS BOOK IS FOR YOU

One of our greatest learnings since writing the first edition is that everyone can lead. When you call a help desk and your issue isn't in the dropdown menu for the person on the other end, they have a choice in that moment to lead or not. We all know how it feels when they do and when they don't.

In our view, any time you face a decision that impacts others, you are leading. Thus, whether you are a student, parent, bus driver, army officer, CEO, grandparent, or citizen of the world, we all have the opportunity to step up and lead.

We wrote this workbook based on the assumption that we are all on a journey to become more authentic leaders. This book is for those who wish to deepen their connection to the magic of who they are so that when they have the opportunity to lead, they will be more likely to step up, lead effectively, and live a meaningful life.

DISCOVERING YOUR AUTHENTIC LEADERSHIP

Becoming an authentic leader is hard work. The process is not much different from becoming a world-class musician or a successful athlete. To become great at anything, you must leverage the unique strengths you were born with, while acknowledging and learning from your shortcomings.

In Bill's case, he had to work very hard to become a leader, enduring disappointing defeats and rejections in high school and early college years. As General Electric's CEO Jeff Immelt describes it, Bill had to make the "leadership journey into [his] own soul" in order to find out who he was, where his real passions lie, and how he could become more effective as a leader. He didn't have a fieldbook like this one to help him, so he made up a plan as he went along. With the help of his wife Penny, close friends, and some important mentors along the way, Bill not only grew and flourished, but he also captured hard-won lessons along the way. Lessons we share with you here.

After searching for a role model for many years, Bill learned that he could never become a great leader by emulating someone else or by minimizing his shortcomings. As "Director of the Year" Reatha Clark King says, "If you're aiming to be like somebody else, you're being a copycat because you think that's what people want you to do. You'll never be a star with that kind of thinking. But you might be a star—unreplicable—by following your passion."

Many books offer quick fixes or seven easy steps to leadership. Unfortunately, development doesn't work that way. To realize your potential as a leader, you need a systematic plan to support your growth. That's the goal of *The Discover Your True North Fieldbook*: to offer a clear and detailed path to guide your development.

We encourage you to take on as many leadership experiences early in life as you can. Don't sit back and wait for them to come to you. Seek them out! After each experience, process them by returning to your development plan, make necessary changes, and reengage with a clearer sense of your True North. This is a lifelong process. Start now.

As you embark on this journey, consider these fundamental truths:

- *You can discover your authentic leadership right now.*
- *You do not have to be born with the characteristics or traits of a leader.*
- *You do not have to wait for a tap on your shoulder.*
- *You do not have to be at the top of your organization.*
- *You can step up to lead at any point in your life: You're never too young—or too old.*
- *Leadership is a choice, not a title.*

USING THIS FIELDBOOK

This fieldbook offers you a series of exercises encouraging you to delve deep into your life story, discover your passions, and develop into an authentic leader. First, you will explore your life story and its relationship to your leadership. Then, you will examine the leadership experiences you have had thus far in your life, including both challenges and disappointments. To keep you from losing your way, we'll also highlight several common patterns that might distract you from realizing your True North.

After a broad review of your life story, we'll ask you to unpack significant crucibles, those searing moments that seem to hold great meaning. By mining your life stories and exploring your crucibles, you begin to uncover unique patterns that help to define who you are, your authentic self.

Next, you will go to work on five key elements of development: self-awareness, values and principles, motivations and sweet spots, support teams, and how to lead an integrated life.

In the final section, we'll ask you to experience what it feels like to make the fundamental shift from "I" to "We," craft a leadership purpose statement, and understand the importance of empowering others in a global context. After completing this work, you'll be ready to create your own Personal Leadership Development Plan (PLDP). This is a dynamic document that you can return to in future years to assess your progress, make any necessary updates, and use as a lifelong guide to remain oriented toward your True North.

SHOULD I WORK WITH OTHERS WHILE USING THIS GUIDE?

Your responses to the exercises and your notes in this fieldbook are personal. However, we do encourage you to share them with trusted others, including mentors, coaches, and members of your support team. Their feedback will be invaluable as you work to develop your PLDP.

As you share your personal story and insights with others, we encourage you to take some risks; experiment with being a bit more vulnerable than perhaps you might ordinarily be. We've found that sharing your story can be incredibly liberating and in fact deepen ties with those you trust.

There are several ways you might use this fieldbook:

1. As an individual, you can complete these exercises and draft your PLDP on your own.

2. You can work through this fieldbook with a group with friends or even new acquaintances. Everyone should complete the exercises individually, and then discuss the insights openly with other members of the group. Then it can be helpful to go back to the exercises and update them, based on others' feedback.

   Your group can be led by a professional facilitator who guides your discussion and keeps the group on track. Or you can create a peer-facilitated group, in which leadership of the group rotates to a different member for each session. Bill pioneered this approach with six-person Leadership Development

Groups (LDGs) in the Authentic Leadership Development course at Harvard Business School.

3. To enhance your learning, you can also use *The Discover Your True North Fieldbook* in conjunction with a personal coach or mentor. Experienced partners can help deepen your learning, provide feedback, and add an additional layer of insights and discipline to the process.

4. You can also use this fieldbook with your team at work. As team leader, you can guide your group through the process yourself or enlist a professional team-building consultant or facilitator to enhance the process.

5. You can use this guide along with the text *Discover Your True North* as the basis for a course on leader development, either in an academic setting or in an organization. This material is flexible enough to support leaders at all stages in their careers: young leaders, including college and graduate students; midcareer leaders; leaders at the top of their organizations; and even very experienced leaders perhaps embarking on the third phase of their journeys after having completed their principal leadership roles.

In the case of a larger group, you may need a professor, teacher, or leadership development professional to help structure the material and lead the group. Nick has spent much of his time working with organizations doing just that with great success. Many others have used this book as the backbone for college, MBA, and executive courses on leadership.

A FINAL WORD TO USERS OF THIS FIELDBOOK

As you embark on this journey of self-discovery, let us offer our personal welcome. We encourage you to be as open and honest as possible when completing these exercises. The more truthful and vulnerable you are, the greater the impact of this work. Have the courage to explore your life deeply, to understand who you are as a magnificent human being, to discover where you really fit in this world, how you can use your leadership to impact others in a positive way, and to leave a lasting legacy that you'll be proud of.

We have witnessed deep and lasting transformation in leaders who have taken this journey as they shaped their twenty-first century authentic organizations and institutions. Whether they were leading in business, government, education, or religion, they discovered that the journey was not only about becoming more authentic themselves, but about empowering everyone they touch to become authentic leaders as well.

Your dedication to discovering your True North will make this world a better and richer place for us all.

April 2015   Welcome,
                                                                                   BILL
                                                                                   NICK
                                                                                   SCOTT

Introduction
Why Authentic Leadership Development?

> Something ignited in my soul . . . And I went my
> own way, deciphering that burning fire.
> —*Pablo Neruda*

Why is it important for you to become an authentic leader?

Leading in the twenty-first century is vastly different from leading in the twentieth century. People in organizations have changed dramatically—to the point where many will no longer tolerate the classic "command and control leaders" of the last century. Nor are they impressed by charismatic leaders who whose leadership is based primarily on personal ego.

Over the past 50 years, many of us worked for powerful leaders who seemed to know where they were going, only to discover later that they were leading us down destructive paths, or that they were in it mostly for themselves and were largely unconcerned with our well-being. Organizations expected us to be loyal to these leaders and wait in line for our turn to lead, if it ever came. And then we learned that our loyalty was not returned, as many lost their pensions and health care. As a consequence, we lost trust in our leaders. Similarly, many of us were dazzled by charismatic leaders who impressed everyone with their charm, yet went off the deep end when the world didn't bend to their personal whims.

People in organizations today seek authentic leaders whom they can trust, but they are not so easily fooled or so quick to offer their loyalty. Many are knowledge workers who often know more than their bosses. They want the opportunity to step up and have an impact now. They are willing to work extremely hard, but will do so only for an organization whose purpose they believe in, as they are seeking meaning and significance in their work. They are willing to trust their leaders only if they prove themselves worthy of their trust.

If you want to be *effective* as a leader today, then you must be *authentic*. If you are not authentic, the best people won't want to work with you, and they won't give you their best work.

What do authentic and effective leaders do?

- They readily align people around a common purpose that inspires them to peak performance.
- They unite people around a common set of values so that everyone knows precisely what is expected.
- They empower others to step up and lead so that people throughout the organization are highly motivated and give their best.
- They are in constant dialogue with all constituencies; as leaders, they bear the responsibility of engaging not only shareholders, but customers, employees, and communities as well.

This is not easy. It is the hard side of leadership.

The easy side of leadership is getting the short-term numbers right. Many smart people can figure out how to do that. It is much more difficult to get people aligned, empowered, and committed to serve a broad set of constituencies.

Being *authentic* as a leader creates a virtuous cycle. The very best people will want to work with you, and as a result, performance will be superior, and you will be able to take on ever greater challenges.

The bottom line is this: In the twenty-first century, without authentic leaders, there will be no sustained effectiveness in organizations.

With authentic leaders, the possibilities are unlimited.

WHAT IS AN AUTHENTIC LEADER?

Authentic leaders have discovered their True North and live it to align people around a shared purpose by empowering others to lead authentically in order to create value for all stakeholders.

Discover Your True North Fieldbook is about mining your life story for deep insights, uncovering the unique gifts that you bring to the world, clarifying your core values, and knowing the underlying purpose of your leadership.

This journey is not about style. This is a common misconception. Authentic leadership is about the deeper you; by knowing and living from your leadership purpose and core values, you are able to let go of seeing yourself as one type of leader (strategic, tactical, introverted, extroverted, etc.). You begin to realize that who you are, your True North, gives you the flexibility to excel in a wide range of situations, all while being true to your authentic self.

Aligning others around a shared purpose and values becomes possible when you can see and feel the connection of your own purpose and values to those of your organization. This enables others to really trust you, increase engagement, and produce higher levels of performance.

This does not mean you have to be perfect. Far from it. Like all of us, you can have your weaknesses and be subject to the full range of human frailties, mistakes, and still be a successful authentic leader. In fact, by acknowledging your shortcomings and admitting your errors, you will connect with people and empower them.

Empowering others to lead is the final element of authentic leadership development. As we stated earlier, true leaders help others become more authentic. Our success is ultimately measured by the ability of others to discover their True North.

HOW WILL THIS FIELDBOOK HELP YOU BECOME AN AUTHENTIC LEADER?

To develop as an authentic leader, you start by reviewing your life story and mining it for patterns and inspiration. You anchor your current leadership profile by reviewing past experiences with leading in order to learn from them. You explore common reasons why leaders lose their way by being an imposter, rationalizer, glory seeker, loner, or shooting star. You identify and unpack significant life crucibles to discover how they influence and shape who you are and how you lead. These elements are covered in Part One of this fieldbook.

Part Two focuses on several elements that define the True North compass:

- *Leading with self-awareness* requires you to ask for tough feedback, be vulnerable, and have compassion for yourself—the cornerstone of authentic leader development.
- *Leading through values* asks you to gain some clarity about your core values, leadership principles, and ethical boundaries.

- *Leading from your sweet spot* encourages you to define when you are at your best by discerning patterns of essential strengths and passions.
- *Leading with wisdom from others* requires you to confront the raw truth—you don't have to go it alone—by encouraging you to conduct an audit of your personal support team.
- *Leading in all parts of your life* demands that you show up the same in every domain of your life and encourages you to define what it really means to live an integrated life.

Part Three focuses on authentic leadership in action. It moves from leading with purpose to empowering others in your organization by selecting the appropriate leadership style to fit the situation. We also explore what it takes to lead in a global context.

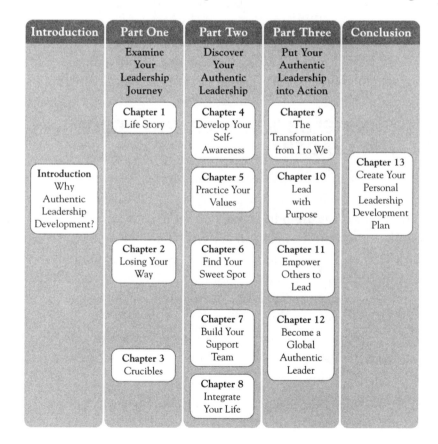

Introduction	Part One	Part Two	Part Three	Conclusion
	Examine Your Leadership Journey	Discover Your Authentic Leadership	Put Your Authentic Leadership into Action	
	Chapter 1 Life Story	**Chapter 4** Develop Your Self-Awareness	**Chapter 9** The Transformation from I to We	
Introduction Why Authentic Leadership Development?		**Chapter 5** Practice Your Values	**Chapter 10** Lead with Purpose	**Chapter 13** Create Your Personal Leadership Development Plan
	Chapter 2 Losing Your Way	**Chapter 6** Find Your Sweet Spot	**Chapter 11** Empower Others to Lead	
		Chapter 7 Build Your Support Team	**Chapter 12** Become a Global Authentic Leader	
	Chapter 3 Crucibles	**Chapter 8** Integrate Your Life		

We conclude by asking you to summarize and integrate everything you've learned in this guide by preparing your own Personal Leadership Development Plan.

YOUR IDEA OF LEADERSHIP

This fieldbook is for anyone interested in becoming more authentic, whether you are currently in a formal leadership position or not, if you plan to lead in the future, or even if you don't typically think of yourself as a leader.

Consider these contrasting examples:

"From my earliest days I have been fascinated with leadership," said Kevin Sharer, CEO of Amgen. "When somebody asked me at 10 years old, 'What do you want to do when you grow up?' I said, 'I just want to be in charge.'"

"I don't think other people think of me as a leader," said David Kelley, founder of IDEO. "'Leader' is a funny word for me. You see, I'm a collaborator. If there is a problem, I call all the smart people I know and get them in a room and have them figure it out."

How about you? How do you think of yourself as a leader?

INTRODUCTORY EXERCISE 1:
LEADERSHIP IMAGES IN YOUR LIFE

You first learn about leadership and leaders by watching others. These examples offer patterns from which to learn. They are the raw material from which to construct the conceptions of leadership you carry into your work and your life.

The purpose of this exercise is to call to mind what you already know about leading, those implicit theories of leadership you've developed by watching others.

Think of five leaders, past or present, whom you have admired. Write their names below, and then answer for yourself the questions that follow.

1. _Ronald Reagan_   _Colin Powell_
2. _Mike kracc_   _Ant_
3. _Reagan_

4. _____

5. _____

Which of these leaders have had the greatest impact on your conceptions of leadership?

1. _____

2. _____

3. _____

4. _____

5. _____

What specific examples of leading stand out in your mind for each of these leaders?

1. _____

2. _____

3. _____

4. _____

5. _____

Which three of these leaders do you consider to be authentic?

1. _____

2. _____

3. _____

What reservations or concerns might you have about following each one?

1. _____

2. _____

3. _____

4. _____

5. _____

How did the context in which each of them led differ from what you face today?

1. _____

2. _____

3. _____

4. _____

5. _____

What qualities, if any, of these three leaders would you like to emulate?

1. _____

2. _____

3. _____

What qualities, if any, would you like to avoid?

1. _____

2. _____

3. _____

NO LEADER IS PERFECT

The biographies of those most often placed on the "best leaders" lists can be surprising at times. Even the most widely admired leaders have very human weaknesses: notable failures as well as successes, startling inconsistencies in relationships or behaviors, and even times of intense struggle with their core values and principles. These struggles do not disqualify anyone from being a source of inspiration, a role model for others, or a teacher. Indeed, leaders, teachers, and mentors must first know and understand their personal developmental needs in order to help you work on yours.

INTRODUCTORY EXERCISE 2:
YOUR PREPARATION FOR LEADING

The purpose of this exercise is to establish a starting point for your work with this fieldbook.

What are the most important qualities you bring to leading?

1. _____
2. _____
3. _____
4. _____
5. _____

All good leaders are continuously developing. Which of your leadership qualities would you like to develop further?

1. _____
2. _____
3. _____
4. _____
5. _____

It is important to keep in mind those qualities that you want to work on. This fieldbook is intended to help you fulfill your aspirations to become a more authentic and effective leader. No one can give you the leadership qualities you seek. You already have them within you. This guide is designed to help you gain a clearer understanding of what they are, identify those aspects of yourself that you like and want to embrace, as well as those that you don't necessarily like and want to change.

LEARNING FROM YOUR LEADERSHIP JOURNEY

In Part One, you will begin your leadership journey. You will venture beyond standard signposts of leadership by examining your life story, learning from times when you lost your way, and unpacking significant life crucibles.

Part One

Examine Your Leadership Journey

> When you're in trouble and all your defenses get stripped away,
> you realize what matters and who matters. That's when you
> need to get back to your roots and to your values.
> —*David Gergen, counselor to four U.S. presidents*

Your life story provides the very foundation for your leadership. Your development as an authentic leader begins by analyzing your story and most formative experiences. As you reflect on your past, you will develop tools to see yourself more clearly, understand your leadership achievements, and embrace your goals for future development.

In Part One of this guide, we begin with your life story.

Chapter 1 Life Story
Chapter 2 Losing Your Way
Chapter 3 Crucibles

1

Life Story

We are the mosaic of all our experiences.
—*Kevin Sharer, chairman and CEO, Amgen*

The process of becoming a True North leader begins by unpacking the fundamental question: Who are you?

When you first meet someone and they say, "So tell me a little bit about yourself," how do you respond? If you are like most of us, you share selected highlights of your life story. In many ways then, we *are* the stories we tell others about ourselves.

In this chapter we ask you to reflect on your life to gain a better understanding of who you are. You will be exploring how various aspects of your story fit together to define you as a unique individual. This is the starting point for gaining greater self-awareness and for understanding what your life and your leadership are all about.

In the 125 interviews we conducted with authentic leaders for *True North* and the additional 30 we added preparing this revision, leaders consistently told us that they found their purpose for leadership by mining their life stories. Having a clear sense of their personal narratives enabled them to remain grounded and stay focused on their True North.

These leaders did not define themselves by a list of characteristics, traits, or styles. Although some tried to emulate great leaders early in their lives, they soon learned that attempting to mimic others did not improve their effectiveness as leaders.

Some interviewees did not see themselves as leaders at all, even though they had been identified by others as exemplary leaders. Instead, they viewed themselves as people who wanted to make a difference and who inspired others to join them in pursuing common goals. By understanding and framing their life stories, they found their passion to lead and were able to discover their True North.

EXERCISE 1.1:
YOUR PATH OF LIFE

In this first exercise, you are going to draw the path of your life to date. See Figure 1.1 for an example of what this might look like. On the facing page is a workspace for drawing your own path. Label the lower left corner of the page "Birth" and the upper right "Present Day." Begin drawing your life's path from one corner to the other.

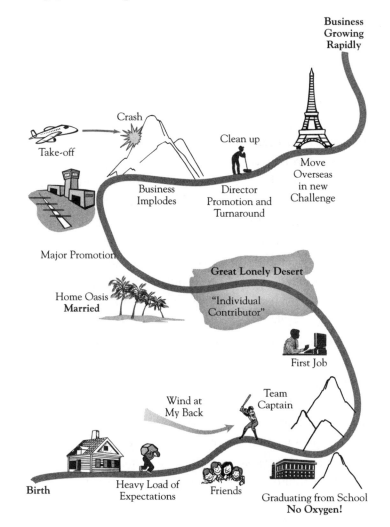

Figure 1.1   Path of Life Example

Your Path of Life

Let the terrain of your journey be unique to who you are. Include mountains and valleys, cities and wilderness, forks, bridges, and cliffs.

Add in houses, buildings, and so on along the way, each representing places you have lived or worked. Likewise, indicate key people and important events with pictures or a diagram along or across the path.

Add representations for your family, work, hobbies, spiritual life . . . anything that is meaningful to you.

Be creative and allow your story to unfold in front of you.

Looking at the path, divide your life story into four or five chapters marked by major changes or critical transitions in your journey. Give each chapter a descriptive title and add it to your path.

LEARNING FROM YOUR LIFE STORY

The story of your life is not your life; it's your story.

—*John Barth, Novelist*

When trying to discover our authentic selves, a good place to start is to examine our life stories. We are largely the stories we tell about ourselves. Stories are the way we capture our experiences in a way that we can understand and in a format that we can communicate to others.

However, as you might have experienced when attempting to draw your path of life, it's not quite that simple. As novelist John Barth reminds us, these "stories" are *not* our lives; they are our stories. They are social constructions, and as such, they have a great deal of play in them. There is no one single, true, and right story of our life.

You've no doubt heard the saying: "You are the author of your life." Look at the path of life you just drew in Exercise 1.1. Now take a few minutes to reflect on the following questions:

- Which story did you ultimately choose to tell when you "authored" this version of your life?
- How did you decide what to include and not to include?
- What's missing and why?

- Imagine all possible versions you considered when drawing your path of life.
    - Which one reflects the *real* you?
    - What can you learn about yourself by reflecting on the version you ultimately decided to draw here today?
- What audience did you have in mind when drawing this version of your life?
- Would the path you drew look any different if you knew someone else would see it?
- How different might it look if you were drawing it for your best friend? Your boss/teacher? Your parents? Your partner? A prospective employer? A prospective date? A newspaper reporter?

Our life stories are just that; they are stories—personal narratives constructed out of recollections from our past. And since our memories are far from perfect, we have a great deal of freedom in how we author the stories of our life. Context matters. Who we are and whom we plan on sharing them with greatly influence the stories we tell about ourselves. Of all the possible stories we might construct about ourselves, which are the most useful?

For our purposes, we find it helpful to draw a distinction between telling your story as a hero, a victim, or a knowledgeable bystander. We believe that your story work will be most helpful if you cultivate the perspective of a caring, knowledgeable bystander rather than that of a hero or a victim. If you are a hero, you miss out on what you need to work on. As a victim, you miss out on your strengths. As a knowledgeable bystander, you can be your own best friend or mentor, someone who knows you intimately, doesn't pull any punches, but who is definitely on your side. Adopting this perspective is best when authoring our life stories for purposes of finding our True North.

Now let's shift our focus to the life story of the most important leader in your life: **you**.

EXERCISE 1.2: LEARNING ABOUT YOUR LEADERSHIP

Reviewing your path of life, call to mind those times when you had the opportunity to lead. These can be formal positions of responsibility or simply experiences when you had the privilege of stepping up and influencing others. Choose a leadership experience you are proudest of, one in which you feel you were at your best. In this exercise, put yourself back in that time and describe it as if it were happening to you right now.

Summarize your proudest leadership experience, starting with the general situation.

What was the context or setting?

_____

_____

_____

_____

What triggered your leadership? What caused you to step up and lead?

_____

_____

_____

_____

What was the outcome? What changed in the people, team, or in the organization as a result?

_____

_____

_____

_____

How did you feel . . .

Before stepping up to lead?

_____

_____

When you first stepped up to lead?

_____

_____

When facing the challenges of the situation?

_____

_____

After the results were in?

_____

_____

What insights did you just gain about your leadership as you told this story?

1. _____

2. _____

3. _____

> Telling your story is an important part of authentic leadership development. Writing your story down gives you a point of reference and helps you gain perspective on yourself.

Now let's probe more deeply into this experience when you were at your best so that you can gain even greater insight.

What leadership qualities did you bring to that leadership challenge or situation?

1. _____

2. _____

3. _____

4. _____

5. _____

How did those qualities contribute to the outcome? Link an outcome to each of the qualities you listed above.

My Leadership Quality	*Its Impact on the Outcome*
1.	
2.	
3.	
4.	
5.	

Draw on what you have read in *Discover Your True North* about the dimensions of authentic leadership. Referring to the experience you just related, rate yourself on the following statements using a 1–5 scale (1 = not at all and 5 = very strongly):

Dimension	Rating
I understood my purpose.	
I practiced my values.	
I understood my motivations.	
I used my support team.	
I was an integrated leader.	

Now, be your own mentor.

Turn back to this story again and look at it from the perspective of the leader you have become since that time.

If you were mentoring yourself at that time, what advice would you give?

_____

_____

_____

In the same spirit, make a list for yourself.

One thing you did really well:

_____

One thing you could have done better:

_____

One thing you could try next time:

_____

In this exercise, you've taken an important step in understanding who you are when you are at your best as a leader. This type of structured reflection is an important discipline that lies at the heart of your journey to becoming a more authentic leader.

AUTHENTICITY AND EFFECTIVENESS

How are authenticity and leadership effectiveness related?

There was a unique advertising scheme popular during the late 1970s called *scratch-and-sniff*. Small stickers or cardboard items attached to a product or magazine page were treated with a fragrant coating. When scratched, these items released an odor associated with images of products or messages related to the smell. As human beings, we are born with incredibly sophisticated scratch-and-sniff meters (also known as BS meters). When we meet someone, whether we are aware of it or not, we immediately begin to assess their authenticity.

Are they for real? Am I buying what they're selling? Do I trust this person?

The relationship between authenticity and leadership effectiveness is straightforward. When we scratch and sniff our leaders, to the extent that we judge them to be "real," we are more likely to respect and follow them. It's that simple. Even if we don't agree with their politics, opinions, or necessarily appreciate their style, as long as we deem them to be transparent, trustworthy, and real—authentic—we have established the necessary condition for building a meaningful relationship. Leaders who fail the scratch-and-sniff test rarely succeed.

EXERCISE 1.3:
AUTHENTICITY AND LEADERSHIP EFFECTIVENESS

The purpose of this exercise is to take stock of how you think authenticity affects your leadership.

List three important people in your life. On a scale of 1–5 (1 = fake/fuzzy and 5 = authentic/ real) how do they fare in response to your scratch-and-sniff meter?

1. _____

2. _____

3. _____

Ask three important people in your life how you fare in response to their scratch-and-sniff meters? Record their names and assessments here.

1. _____

2. _____

3. _____

YOUR JOURNEY TO AUTHENTIC LEADERSHIP

Experience is often said to be the best teacher. Experience is, however, not necessarily a kind or clear teacher. Your life story is, in part, a chronicle of your experiences in the world. Comparing early with late chapters, you will notice contrasts. In one chapter, you may have been preparing to lead. In another, you might have focused on leading or simply trying to make your way in the world. Some passages may be marked by education or apprenticeship—times when you were operating in the context of rules that structured and measured your activities. Later chapters may come in a different context, perhaps marked by increased responsibilities with fewer rules and structures.

The interesting thing is that most out-of-classroom experiences are perceived as learning experiences only in retrospect. At any given moment, you will probably not have the feeling that you are preparing or training. You will be in the thick of your life. If you pay attention to the possibilities in each situation or crisis however, every day can be a lesson on your journey to True North.

Now let's look at your life from a slightly different angle. Whereas you told the previous story as if you were experiencing it in real time, now you are going to tell this story in retrospect, from satellite height, surveying the entire arc of your life. Do not limit this reflection to aspects of your career or work-related life. Through our interviews with authentic leaders, we learned that early life experiences were frequently the most formative and were often the most significant contributors to both the type of leaders they became and the formation of their True North.

EXERCISE 1.4: YOUR LIFE STORY

In this exercise, you will explore each chapter of your life story to identify those people, events, and experiences that have had the greatest impact on your identity.

Start by looking back at the chapters you identified in your path of life (Exercise 1.1).

Which people, events, and experiences have had the greatest impact on your life?

_____

_____

_____

_____

Now, let's really squeeze this rock, mine it for all it's worth. Consider each chapter in turn, and use the following questions to guide you through the process of identifying the central lessons of your life. Use the list generated above, insights from your path of life, and anything else that occurs to you during this reflective process.

Begin with your Chapter 1 and use the prompts in Table 1.1 as a guide. Complete Table 1.1.

Table 1.1: The Impact of My Life Story

	Chapter 1	Chapter 2	Chapter 3	Chapter 4	Chapter 5
Chapter title					
The central lesson I take away from this chapter about others/ the world is this:					
The central lesson I take away from this chapter about myself is this:					
If I could go back, here is what I would do differently:					
Critical insights from this chapter of my life still affect me in the following ways:					

Now you are going to look at your story as a whole in an attempt to trace the origins of your leadership. If you haven't yet had the opportunity to lead in a formal way, that's okay. Be creative. Think more broadly. Even if you've never been in a formal position of authority, there have been times in your life when you've noticed something that needed to be done, and you stepped up and influenced others to make it happen. That's leading. The days of narrowly defining leadership as only those actions taken by people in positions of authority are long gone.

Where do you first notice yourself as a leader?

_____

_____

_____

How has this developed over time?

_____

_____

_____

Now focus on those most important people in your life. Consider the impact that parents, siblings, family members, mentors, and friends have had on your inspiration and passion for leadership.

Who has had the greatest influence on your leadership?

_____

_____

_____

EXERCISE 1.5: LAUNCH POINT

As you review your path of life and scan the chapters of your story, where are you right now when it comes to your development as a leader? Whether you feel like you've never led in your life or have a rich résumé behind you, it doesn't matter. We are all works in progress. Our development as leaders is an ongoing, emergent process. To help anchor the foundation for your work in the rest of this book, be as honest as you can with yourself and answer the following questions:

Where are you in your leadership journey (e.g. novice, journeyman, legend)?

_____

_____

_____

How sure are you that you want to lead (e.g., clueless, pretty sure, confident)?

_____

_____

_____

How would you describe yourself as a leader?

_____

_____

_____

BUILDING ON YOUR STORY

The journey to discovering your True North starts by looking in the rearview mirror. Our life experiences provide rich grist for the mill of leader development. We are largely the stories we tell about ourselves. Gaining a deeper understanding and comfort with these narratives is the first step toward developing into a more authentic person and leader.

Laying your whole life out in front of you can be a powerful experience. Rarely do we step back and see the journey we are on. Through the lens of your life story, you can begin to see the wellsprings of your purpose, values, and motivations. Some of these have come from your proudest leadership experience; others may flow from major life events that seem to have no direct bearing on leadership. As the late leadership guru Warren Bennis reminds us, "The process of becoming a leader is much the same as the process of becoming an integrated human being." This process begins and ends with the stories of our lives.

In the next two chapters, we will delve even deeper into your story by asking you to explore some potentially uncomfortable subjects: the hazards of leadership and the lessons of adversity. It takes courage, but exploring how you might "lose your way" and revisiting life's most difficult experiences can bring both insight and clarity to your True North.

KEY TAKEAWAYS

- We are the stories we tell about ourselves.
- Learning from our experiences holds the key to our development as leaders.
- To learn best from your story, it is important to step away from both the hero's view and from the victim's view of your life. Adopting the perspective of an objective observer increases the likelihood that we'll see our true selves.
- Your past leadership experiences point the way to discovering your potential as an authentic leader.
- Each chapter of your life contains critical lessons that will help you find *your* True North.

SUGGESTED READING

Baldwin, C. Storycatcher: *How the Power of Story Can Change Our Lives*. Novato, Calif.: New World Library, 2005.

Boas, S., and Eilam, G. "What's your story?" A life-story approach to authentic leadership development. *The Leadership Quarterly*, 16, 2005.

Bruner, J. S. *Actual Minds, Possible Selves*. Cambridge, MA: Harvard University Press, 1986.

Franco, C., and Lineback, K. *The Legacy Guide: Capturing the Facts, Memories, and Meaning of Your Life*. New York: Penguin, 2006.

Kahneman, D. "Two Selves" in *Thinking Fast and Slow*. New York: Farrar, Straus and Giroux, 2011.

McCall, M. W., Lombardo, M. M. & Morrison, A. M. *The Lessons of Experience*. Lexington, MA: D. C. Heath, 1988.

Wilson, T. *Redirect: Changing the Stories We Live By*. New York: Little Brown Books, 2011.

2

Losing Your Way

It was as if someone flashed a mirror at me at my absolute worst.
What I saw was horrifying, but it was also a great lesson.
—Doug Baker Jr., chairman and CEO, Ecolab

Leadership development is a journey through challenging terrain. All leaders, even the most authentic ones, face significant hazards on their journeys. Being human, we chase rewards, seek to avoid bad outcomes, and value social acceptance and acclaim. These are normal human tendencies, but when left unchecked, they can sabotage both our personal and professional lives.

Authentic leaders must learn to become aware of and overcome a common pattern of impulses that can lead to problematic behaviors. Leaders who lose their way succumb to the negative temptations of leadership and may even grow to celebrate those very same destructive tendencies that eventually lead to their fall.

The good news is that we can make mistakes and fall prey to these hazards, and still regain our footing and continue on our way. In fact, these mistakes, especially when they come early in our careers, can be important opportunities for development. When recognized for what they are, understanding these potential sources of derailment early in our careers can reduce the likelihood of making major mistakes once we reach positions of greater authority. If we recognize these hazards and invest sufficient efforts to avoid them, we will be less likely to become enmeshed in more deeply destructive patterns and more likely to persevere and emerge as authentic leaders.

ON THE HERO'S JOURNEY

Through our research on authentic leaders, we uncovered a striking feature of their stories. Early chapters fit the pattern of what mythologist Joseph Campbell calls "the hero's journey." Many leaders approach their early career as if they were on the quest of an all-conquering hero, with a primary focus on themselves, their skills, performance, achievements, and rewards.

Transitioning out of the hero's journey feels similar to making that first leap from individual contributor to leader-manager. Most of us earn the privilege of leading by first being great individual contributors. We get hired for our technical expertise in getting a job done . . . by ourselves. Whether it's writing a research paper, creating a slide deck, or running numbers on a spreadsheet, being really good at something often leads to advancement and the opportunity to lead. Therein lies the rub.

The hero's job—doing impressive deeds, facing challenges alone, and gaining notice—may initially seem the best route to success. But acting as a hero is only the first stage we move through on our journey toward becoming authentic leaders. It is a necessary but temporary stage—with its own unique set of risks, temptations, and misbehaviors—a stage most of us experience, but must eventually move beyond.

Falling into the Trap of Becoming a Hero

Many of the perils of the hero stage are well described by Daniel Vasella, CEO of Novartis, in the following interview with *Fortune* magazine:

Once you get under the domination of making the quarter—even unwittingly . . . you'll begin to sacrifice things that are important and may be vital for your company over the long term. The culprit that drives this cycle isn't the fear of failure so much as it is the craving for success . . . For many of us the idea of being a successful manager is an intoxicating one. It is a pattern of celebration leading to belief, leading to distortion. When you achieve good results, you are typically celebrated, and you begin to believe that the figure at the center of all that champagne toasting is yourself. You are idealized by the outside world, and there is a natural tendency to believe that what is written is true.

Leaf, C. "Temptation Is All Around Us." *Fortune*, Nov. 18, 2002

After moving through the hero stage, you enter the first stage of true leadership. Leaders who move beyond the hero stage learn to focus on others, delegate, gain a sense of a larger purpose, foster multiple support networks, and develop mechanisms to keep perspective and stay grounded. They become the kind of people employees and peers trust and want to work with.

During the hero stage of development, you are particularly vulnerable to the five hazards discussed in this chapter. Yet whether you are in the hero stage or think you have already moved on, you always remain vulnerable to the deeply rooted temptations of these powerful traps.

FIVE HAZARDS OF LEADERSHIP DEVELOPMENT

There are five archetypal hazards—common, recognizable patterns of destructive behaviors—that tempt us during the hero stage of our development:

- being an imposter;
- rationalizing;
- glory seeking;
- playing the loner; and
- being a shooting star.

We all see these archetypes in others. The developmental challenge is to recognize them in ourselves.

To some extent, these five hazards grow out of a distinct set of naturally emerging fears that all young leaders face when pursuing a related set of healthy goals. Table 2.1 illustrates some of these goals, as well as those fears that seem to be associated with them. For each fear, we have outlined both a destructive response and a healthy response.

In the sections that follow, we unpack each hazard in turn.

Table 2.1: Healthy Versus Destructive Responses to Normal Goals and Fears

Normal Goal	Natural Fear	Destructive Response	Healthy Response
Wanting respect and rewards from authority	Making mistakes and having one's lack of skill or knowledge exposed	Imposter (work with "Develop Your Self-Awareness")	Self-authored leader
Wanting things to go well	Getting blamed and suffering consequences	Rationalizer (work with "Live Your Values")	Straight shooter
Enjoying shared successes	Not being rewarded enough	Glory seeker (work with "Find Your Sweet Spot")	"We"-focused leader
Thriving in interdependent relationships	Becoming too dependent on others	Loner (work with "Build Your Support Team")	Team leader
Wanting to capitalize on successes for advancement	Falling behind others	Shooting star (work with "Integrate Your Life")	Rising star

Being an Imposter

When they first assume the mantle of leadership, few leaders feel "completely ready." Stepping up to lead often moves us out of our comfort zones. This is a totally natural response when facing any new challenge, particularly one in which you are responsible for others. How you respond to this challenge determines whether or not you'll be experienced as authentic and trustworthy or nervous and political.

When you feel like an imposter, it is difficult to act decisively. You might experience paralyzing doubt that leads to inaction and poor results. If you do not recognize and overcome this hazard, you will likely be tempted to attack your critics and cut yourself off from internal feedback. Because they are frustrated by their inability to influence you, some of your most competent subordinates may move on to greener pastures. Meanwhile, people remaining in the organization are likely to be those who tend to keep their heads down and wait for you to make decisions.

Leaders are vulnerable to becoming imposters if they lack self-awareness. Having acquired power, imposters are uncomfortable and uncertain about how to use it. They are beset with doubts about shouldering the responsibilities of leadership. Because one of an imposter's strengths is besting internal opponents, they often risk becoming paranoid that underlings are out to get them.

Almost everyone experiences doubt about how to handle novel situations. Many of us are also very competitive and feel the need to outshine others in order to stand out in an organization. Worrying about your abilities, questioning whether you can handle a new challenge by yourself, sometimes having to display public confidence when you harbor private doubts, and recognizing a need to develop additional areas of knowledge and skill can all be characteristics of healthy, authentic leaders. It is when these doubts themselves become the overriding driver of behavior that potentially destructive patterns emerge.

The Imposter

Imposters frequently lack self-awareness and self-esteem. They may have little appetite for self-reflection and consequently defer personal development. They rise through organizational ranks with a combination of cunning and aggression. Imposters use these strategies to achieve positions of power, but then have little sense of how to use that power for the good of the organization. In effect, they have been too busy besting competitors to learn how to lead. Leaders who succumb to this hazard embrace the politics of getting ahead and let no one stand in their way. They are the ultimate political animals, adept at figuring out who their competitors are and then eliminating them one by one.

EXERCISE 2.1: IDENTIFYING THE IMPOSTER

This exercise focuses on recognizing aspects of the imposter in your life story.

Describe a situation where you found it difficult to make decisions because of self-doubt.

_____

_____

_____

What did you think you were not able to do?

_____

_____

_____

How did you feel? What did you think your colleagues' responses would be if you failed?

_____

_____

_____

How did you deal with the situation?

_____

_____

_____

What would you do differently today if you found yourself in a similar position?

_____

_____

_____

In this exercise, you have identified an episode in your journey when you faced a major challenge to your self-awareness. We have never met leaders who were not well acquainted with self-doubt and tempted at times to represent themselves as different from who they really were.

In Table 2.2, circle any characterizations that you identify with your present leadership.

If you circled examples in the Early Warning and/or Red Alert columns, you will want to pay particular attention to Chapter 4, Develop Your Self-Awareness.

Table 2.2: Indicators of the Imposter

Healthy Approaches to Dealing with Doubt	Early Warning Signs	Red Alerts
I make the best decisions possible in a timely fashion.	My decision making becomes protracted as I seek perfect solutions.	I experience paralyzing doubt when making decisions.
I measure my capabilities against those needed to achieve my goals.	I measure competitors' capabilities rather than my own.	Political infighting takes priority over developing myself.
I seek actionable and appropriate developmental feedback.	I put off seeking feedback.	I am hostile to developmental feedback.
I take input from a wide range of others, and then make my own best decision.	I seek input only when I know what I'm going to hear.	I rarely ask others for advice.

Rationalizing

When you are being drawn off course by rationalizing, you tend to blame external forces or others when things do not go your way. At first, you might deny that problems actually exist. When you do acknowledge their existence and your responsibility for them, your instinct is often to cover up the problems or seek to diminish their seriousness. You may not be willing to acknowledge even to yourself that things could get worse. If rationalizing becomes a habit, it is progressively more difficult to step up and take responsibility for problems or failures. In times like these, others judge your actions and decide whether they are true to your values, whether your actions match what you say you believe.

When leading, if you continue to rationalize outcomes, others in your organization may also begin to rationalize their problems rather than face up to them. This pattern can quickly spread throughout your group or organization. If it does, holding anyone accountable becomes nearly impossible. At that point, rationalizers often respond by transmitting greater pressure to subordinates instead of modulating it appropriately. When increased pressure fails to produce desired results, you may resort to short-term strategies, such as cutting funding for research, growth initiatives, or organization building in order to hit short-term goals. You might be tempted to borrow from the future to make today's numbers look good, or even stretch accounting rules. All along, you justify these moves by rationalizing that you can make it up in the future. Ultimately, leaders who do not overcome the hazard of rationalizing become victims of their own rationalizations.

Leaders who are not clear about their values, leadership principles, and ethical boundaries are particularly vulnerable to the hazards of rationalization. Lacking that clarity, with no sound boundaries around their behaviors, rationalizers often convince themselves that the ends justify the means. Ultimately, the ends are not achieved, though, and the means do not constitute authentic leadership.

It is really hard to consistently live up to your values and aspirations. All leaders have to make tough choices between competing values, and no one gets it right all the time. Slowing things down to the point where you at least recognize the tension in competing values or principles, and then doing your best to reconcile these tensions in an intentional way, is the true mark of an authentic leader. But if this process turns into rationalizing, you may lose your way.

The Rationalizer

Rationalizers are unable to admit their mistakes for fear of being considered failures or of losing their jobs. As a result of their inability to accept responsibility for setbacks and failures, they rationalize problems away instead of facing reality. These rationalizations often lead to distortions and encourage others to rationalize as well.

EXERCISE 2.2: IDENTIFYING THE RATIONALIZER

This exercise focuses on identifying times when you rationalized your behavior.

Describe a situation where you rationalized failing to live up to your values.

_____

_____

_____

What were the values you were working around?

_____

_____

_____

How did you feel at the time?

_____

_____

_____

What happened as a result?

_____

_____

_____

If you found yourself in a similar position today, what would you do in order to act differently?

_____

_____

_____

In Table 2.3, circle those characterizations you most identify with when facing a difficult decision.

If you circled examples in the Early Warning and/or Red Alert columns, you will want to pay particular attention to Chapter 5, Practice Your Values.

Table 2.3: Indicators of the Rationalizer

Healthy Approaches to Making Difficult Decisions	Early Warning Signs	Red Alerts
I accept mixed outcomes from my decisions.	I often find it difficult to learn from mistakes and move on.	I am unable to acknowledge mistakes.
I weigh means and ends when making decisions.	I push the envelope of acceptable ways to achieve a goal.	I will do anything to achieve my goals; the ends justify the means.
I take appropriate risks and find that some opportunities pass me by.	I borrow from the future to make ends meet because I take inappropriate risks.	I have put others at risk in order to achieve a personal goal.
I occasionally operate in crisis mode.	I operate best in crisis mode.	I operate in continual states of crisis requiring short-term strategies.
I take responsibility for mistakes and fix them, encouraging others to do the same.	I find that problems and mistakes are orphans, without clear responsibility.	I operate in an accountability vacuum.
I communicate about both my challenges and my achievements.	I polish the upside to distract from problems.	I hide problems and bury bodies.

Glory Seeking

I (Scott) distinctly recall a time when I asked my 12-year-old daughter the classic question, "What do you want to be when you grow up?" Without skipping a beat, she shouted, "I want to be famous!" "Okay," I responded. "Famous for what? Do you want to be a world-class musician?" (She played the drums.) "Or perhaps a professional athlete?" (She played soccer.) "No," she repeated, "I just want to be famous." As she blissfully skipped off in the way only a 12-year-old can do, it hit me: In the age of reality TV, where Paris Hilton and Kim Kardashian are known only for . . . well, for being famous, my daughter had already succumbed to the constant onslaught of social media. Her highest aspiration in life was not to be a doctor or a teacher, but rather to be famous—the ultimate seduction that lies at the heart of "glory seeking."

Glory seekers are leaders who are more concerned with their status and reputation than they are with building teams or organizations that create sustainable value.

You risk becoming a glory seeker when you are motivated primarily by money, fame, power, and glory. If you let the external world define your success and harbor a deep hunger for such recognition, you may find that your inner drive is constantly focused on obtaining more—more money, more adulation, more recognition, more prestige, or more power over others.

Research professor and noted author Brené Brown argues that we live in a "culture of scarcity." We are constantly bombarded by messages implying that we are "not enough"—not beautiful enough, not smart enough, not wealthy enough. Of course, in our more lucid moments, we understand that there will always be others who are better looking, more intelligent, and have more money; that there is no rational end to this "not enough" game. And yet, a deeper interpretation of this powerful message is that we are simply *not enough*. We have internalized the idea that it is not enough to be ourselves because we are lacking in some way—in our looks, intelligence, or wealth—to keep us from belonging or from being loved.

It is this logic behind our culture of scarcity that drives the glory seeker in all of us. Glory seeking is the shadow expression of leaders who are unable to balance their intrinsic and extrinsic motivations and who fail to link their motivations with their capabilities. Falling prey to this hazard often results from a lack of self-love and an unhealthy need to seek external recognition to fill a void within.

The Glory Seeker

People who seek glory are driven primarily by extrinsic motivations, such as a need for acclaim. Glory seekers are defined by an overwhelming need for external approval and validation. Money, fame, glory, and power are not only concrete markers of success, but for glory seekers, they are essential aspects of personal self-worth.

EXERCISE 2.3: IDENTIFYING THE GLORY SEEKER

This exercise focuses on identifying times in your life story when you behaved like a glory seeker.

Complete the following sentence: "I am not _____ enough."

How might your desire to be _____ enough (fill in the blank) drive the glory seeker in you?

_____

_____

_____

Now describe a situation when you felt an overwhelming need for external recognition or financial rewards to enhance your self-worth.

_____

_____

_____

What did it feel like at the time?

_____

_____

_____

How did you deal with your desire for glory?

_____

_____

_____

What would you do today if you found yourself in a similar position?

_____

_____

_____

In Table 2.4, circle those characterizations that define the role that seeking external rewards plays in your life.

If you circled examples in the Early Warning and/or Red Alert columns, you will want to pay particular attention to Chapter 6, Find Your Sweet Spot.

Table 2.4: Indicators of the Glory Seeker

Healthy Approaches to Seeking External Rewards in Your Life	Early Warning Signs	Red Alerts
I maintain a balanced portfolio of desires and motivations.	I have difficulty weighing tangible against intangible desires and motivations.	I often choose fame, power, or glory over any other.
I take on even drudge work in order to achieve my goals.	I defer meaningful or satisfying motivations out of necessity.	I often find myself burned out and dread going to work.
I work toward shared goals with others, even when those goals are not all my own.	I work with others toward goals so long as those goals match my own.	I do not work with others because they do not have my interests at heart.
I ensure that others get appropriate credit for their contributions to my success.	I let others look out for their own credit when contributing to my success.	I overstate my contributions to my success.

Playing the Loner

You know you are falling into the trap of playing the loner when you tend to avoid forming close relationships, do not seek out mentors, and do not have a rich support network of friends, colleagues, and peers. Being a loner is endemic among many leaders we have encountered. Many get promoted to positions of increased power by relying on their individual capabilities, ambition, and a drive that may be born out of insecurity.

It is natural in the heroic stage of your journey to think of leadership as a solitary pursuit, but it is also perilous. In a competitive world where we are largely evaluated on our individual merits, it stands to reason that aspiring leaders would take care to hoard their own resources, champion their own ideas, and trust only their own judgment.

But therein lies the danger, as loners can easily fall into a self-reinforcing trap. Under pressure, they retreat to the bunker when results are elusive and criticism surfaces.

As loners, they have few personal support structures in place to help them through challenging times. As a result, they become overly rigid in pursuing objectives, not recognizing that being a loner only decreases the likelihood of achieving their goals. Meanwhile, their teams and organizations can unravel, and their personal lives are at risk of crumbling, just when they most need the support of family and friends.

The Loner

When we become loners, we cut ourselves off from much-needed feedback. Yet without wise counsel, loners are prone to losing perspective and becoming rigid, which will lead to major mistakes.

EXERCISE 2.4: IDENTIFYING THE LONER

This exercise focuses on identifying times in your life when you acted like a loner.

Describe a situation when you retreated into yourself rather than asking for counsel and advice.

_____

_____

_____

What did you feel at the time?

_____

_____

_____

How did you deal with your feelings of isolation and stress?

_____

_____

_____

What would you do differently now if you found yourself confronted by a similar situation?

_____

_____

_____

In Table 2.5, circle those tendencies you recognize in yourself.

If you circled examples in the Early Warning and/or Red Alert columns, you will want to pay particular attention to Chapter 7, Build Your Support Team.

Table 2.5: Indicators of the Loner

Healthy Approaches to Seeking External Rewards in Your Life	Early Warning Signs	Red Alerts
I seek input from others and then make up my own mind.	I avoid input from others and avoid working with groups or sharing responsibilities.	I do not accept input from others.
I take input and gauge the wind, but then look only forward after I make decisions.	I make impulsive decisions that seem to come out of the blue.	I make impulsive decisions that are out of touch with others.
I have a mix of long-term and short-term work relationships.	I sometimes have difficulty seeking help from a mentor or peer.	I often feel a sense of isolation.
My relationships are characterized by the free exchange of ideas.	My relationships are dominated by the question of who is doing what for whom.	I have few or no close associates.
I am effective at different kinds of work in several different contexts.	For me, being productive requires "getting away from it all."	I seek out an isolated work environment.

Being a Shooting Star

At times of rapid change and advancement, leaders risk becoming shooting stars, burning brightly and moving fast, then suddenly and unexpectedly crashing back to Earth. If your life centers entirely on your career and you are always on the go, traveling incessantly to get ahead, you are at risk of becoming a shooting star whose life is spiraling out of control.

The increasing pace of organizational life, fueled by information technology, globalization, and hyper-competition, creates a growing demand for talented people interested in being on the fast track. High achievement and top leadership posts often go to those who start early and run fast.

As an emerging leader, you risk becoming a shooting star just when you are moving up so rapidly in your career that you never have time to learn from your mistakes. When you move on after only a year or two in any job, and never pause to make an honest assessment of your leadership, you never confront the consequences of your past. When you see problems of your own making coming back to haunt you, your response will probably be to become anxious rather than to summon the determination to apply the painful lessons of your experience.

Because you are viewed as a star, you have tempting levers to pull. For example, you can threaten your employer with a move to another organization if you are not promoted. If you do this often enough, one day you will eventually find yourself in a high-level position where you are overwhelmed by an intractable set of problems. At this point, you will be prone to impulsive or even irrational decisions because you have no grounding in your life that enables you to cope with these problems in a rational matter. This is the point when shooting stars flame out, come crashing down, and are finally forced to face their own reality.

When you sense an urgency to escape from your current challenges and find a new position, this is the time to assess whether you are moving so fast that you have lost touch with your inner compass and are at risk of losing your bearings.

The Shooting Star

Leaders who fall into the shooting star trap lack the grounding of an integrated life. They rarely make time for family, friendships, their communities, or even themselves. Much-needed sleep and exercise are continually deferred. Stress mounts as they run ever faster, often to the point where they risk flaming out.

EXERCISE 2.5: IDENTIFYING THE SHOOTING STAR

This exercise focuses on identifying times in your life when you were at risk of becoming a shooting star.

Describe the run-up to a situation in which you were becoming a shooting star and what happened in that situation.

_____

_____

_____

What were the main feelings you had at the time?

_____

_____

_____

What did you do to recover?

_____

_____

_____

What would you do now to avoid the risk of burning out if you were confronted by a similar situation today?

_____

_____

_____

In Table 2.6, circle any patterns you recognize in yourself.

If you circled examples in the Early Warning and/or Red Alert columns, you will want to pay particular attention to Chapter 8, Integrate Your Life.

Table 2.6: Indicators of the Shooting Star

Healthy Approaches to Seeking External Rewards in Your Life	*Early Warning Signs*	*Red Alerts*
I commit to achieving my goals.	To achieve my goals, I carve away other parts of my life, such as weekends or vacations.	I sometimes feel exhausted when working toward my goals.
I build my capacity through continuous learning.	I focus on finding opportunities to do what I already do best.	My best sometimes feels stale or old.
I look for the right position and level to match my capabilities.	I look for new challenges before my current ones have been resolved.	I have moved rapidly from job to job and assignment to assignment.
I bring out the best in others as I bring out the best in myself.	I focus on being seen at my best at all times.	I bring out my best even when it drives down others around me.
I am devoted to my work.	My work contributes to my losing contact with friends and puts strains on my family life.	I do not know my neighbors, my children's friends, or my partner.

EXERCISE 2.6: CONDUCT A PREMORTEM: HOW MIGHT YOUR STRENGTHS BECOME WEAKNESSES?

You've probably heard of the medical term *postmortem*—a procedure where physicians examine a dead body to determine the cause of death. But have you ever heard of conducting a *premortem*—brainstorming ahead of time to imagine the most likely cause of death?

Morbid terms, to be sure. However, both phrases have worked their way into management circles. When projects fail, postmortems are conducted to discern why. Similarly, research has shown that "projective hindsight"—imagining that an event has already occurred—can improve our ability to predict causes of future outcomes by almost 30 percent.

We're going to ask you to conduct a premortem on yourself to determine the most likely cause of how you might lose your way by combining this technique with the time-tested wisdom that "our strengths can often become weaknesses." Imagining the most likely scenario for your derailment is not only a potent antidote to narcissism, but conducting an honest premortem on yourself is also a powerful remedy for each of the five hazards in this chapter.

List 3–5 of your greatest strengths as a leader (or a person).

_____

_____

_____

_____

_____

For each of these, how might they become a weakness?

_____

_____

_____

_____

_____

As a result, what is the most likely scenario for losing your way?

_____

_____

_____

_____

_____

GETTING BACK ON TRACK IS A SOURCE OF STRENGTH

In this chapter, you have begun to see how you might lose your way. Each of us is at risk of being pulled off course from our True North by the pressures and seductions of modern life. All five archetypes for how we might lose our way are in part fueled by a misguided desire to always present ourselves in a favorable light. Following a path dictated primarily by what we think the world wants to see—who we think we *should* be, instead of who we actually *are*—is a sure recipe for disaster.

Being an authentic leader is not about being perfect. Out of her groundbreaking research on shame, Brené Brown reminds us that perfectionism is not the same as striving for excellence or self-improvement. These latter pursuits are healthy goals in line with personal growth; perfectionism focuses on others' perceptions of who we are. According to Brown:

> "Perfectionism is, at its core, about trying to earn approval. Most perfectionists grew up being praised for achievement and performance. Somewhere along the way, they adopted this dangerous and debilitating belief system: 'I am what I accomplish and how well I accomplish it. Please. Perform. Perfect.' Healthy striving is self-focused: How can I improve? Perfectionism is other-focused: What will they think? Perfectionism is a hustle . . . a twenty-ton shield that we lug around, thinking it will protect us, when in fact it's the thing that's really preventing us from being seen." (Brown, p. 29)

If you want to avoid being that imposter who rationalizes the way to glory and ends up alone and burned out, start by gaining a deeper understanding of yourself. You cannot lose your way if you never had one in the first place. In the next chapter, we'll help you "find your way" by exploring your crucibles—those searing moments in life that seem heavily laden with meaning—moments that, when fully understood, become instrumental in helping you find your True North.

KEY TAKEAWAYS

- All leaders are prone to losing their way at one point or another.
- We live in a "culture of scarcity," constantly reminded that we are "not enough."
- We all desire rewards and acceptance from others.
- The five hazards of leadership—being an impostor, rationalizer, glory seeker, loner, or shooting star—spring from this culture of scarcity and an unhealthy relationship with these desires.

- Being authentic is not about being perfect.

- Understanding how our strengths might become weaknesses can be a powerful antidote to losing our way.

- Losing our way is not necessarily fatal; learning from our imperfections determines whether we are in fact losing or finding our way in life.

SUGGESTED READING

Berglas, S. Victims of Their Own Success. In R. B. Kaiser (Ed.), *The Perils of Accentuating the Positive* (pp. 7–96), Tulsa, OK: Hogan Press, 2009.

Brown, B. *Daring Greatly.* New York: Gotham Books, 2012.

Dotlich, D. L., & Cairo, P. C. *Why CEOs Fail.* San Francisco: Jossey-Bass, 2003.

Finkelstein, S. *Why Smart Executives Fail and What You Can Learn from Their Mistakes.* New York: Portfolio, 2003.

Fiorina, C. *Tough Choices.* New York: Portfolio, 2006.

Goleman, D. *Destructive Emotions.* New York: Bantam Books, 2003.

Hill, L. *Becoming a Manager: How New Managers Master the Challenges of Leadership.* Boston: Harvard Business School Publishing, 2003.

Klein, Gary. "Performing a project premortem." *Harvard Business Review* 85.9, pp: 18–19, 2007.

Lombardo, M. M. & Eichinger, R. W. *Preventing Derailment: What to Do before It's too Late.* Greensboro, NC: Center for Creative Leadership, 1999.

McCall, M. W. Jr. *High Flyers.* Cambridge, MA: Harvard Business School Press, 1998.

Mitchel, D. J, Russo, J. E. and Pennington, N. "Back to the Future: Temporal Perspective in the Explanation of Events." *Journal of Behavioral Decision Making*, 2, 25–38, 1989.

Maccoby, M. *The Productive Narcissist.* Los Angeles: Broadway Books, 2003.

Van Velsor, E., and Leslie, J. B. "Why Executives Derail: Perspectives across Time and Cultures." *Academy of Management Review*, 9, 62–72, 1995.

3

Crucibles

When heated directly by fire, the fire of trial, the heat of disease,
Infernos of grief and penury . . .
Can we hold under the terror, the torment of transforming, under forging,
Until we are bearers of light, torches, for sufferance, for illumining oblivion?
—*Susan Deborah King, from "Crucible," in* One-Breasted Woman

Chapter 1 introduced the central notion that "we are largely the stories we tell about ourselves." In Chapter 2, we asked you to practice some "projective hindsight" to imagine how you might lose your way in hopes that, in fact, you wouldn't "lose it," but rather "find it" and increase the chances that you'll stay on course. Here, we ask you to return to your life story, this time scanning it for particularly salient experiences that seem heavily laden with meaning. We call these crucibles.

Life is chock-full of potentially rich developmental experiences. But not all of it. In fact, most of our waking hours are pretty boring. Our challenge here is to identify those times that seem most interesting and squeeze them for all they're worth. As you embark on this chapter in your journey toward authentic leadership, consider the following two questions:

- What events, relationships, or periods in your life have had the greatest impact on who you are?
- What did you learn from these crucibles?

It can be hard to gain insight and learn from periods of productive ferment, difficulties, and challenges when we are in the midst of them. Yet it is often during the most difficult times that we have the opportunity to confront who we are at the deepest level and realize what our lives and our leadership are all about.

CRUCIBLES

In their book *Geeks and Geezers,* authors Warren Bennis and Robert Thomas describe crucibles as intense experiences that test us to our very limits. Crucibles force us to look at ourselves, examine our character and values in a new light, and come to grips with who we really are. "The skills required to conquer adversity and emerge stronger and more committed than ever," they conclude, "are the same ones that make for extraordinary leaders."

Many crucibles involve pain and loss. Examples from your professional life might include confronting a difficult challenge at work, receiving critical feedback, getting passed over for promotion, or losing a job. Experiencing a divorce, illness, or death of a loved one are examples of highly consequential events in our personal lives that often qualify as potential crucibles.

> To a chemist, a crucible is a vessel in which substances are heated to high temperatures in order to trigger a chemical transformation, as in the case of the refinement of gold ore or a steel refinery's blast furnace. The crucible is an ancient technology and has yielded rich literary references over time, ranging from the refiner's fire of the Old Testament prophets, to the metaphor and techniques of alchemists, to Arthur Miller's play about the Salem Witch Trials, *The Crucible.*

While often painful, crucibles don't necessarily have to be negative events. Getting accepted into a prestigious school, winning a big game or competition, or truly leading for the first time are all significant experiences with the potential to fundamentally shape who we are. Particularly powerful relationships with mentors, elders, or personal heroes can also play an important role in our development. These too might qualify as a crucible. Any event or period of your life that forces deep self-reflection, that causes you to question your most basic assumptions, values, and worldview, has the potential to qualify as a crucible.

Shortly after the end of the 2004 college basketball season, Duke University's legendary men's basketball coach Mike Krzyzewski (aka: Coach K) unexpectedly faced one of the most important decisions of his life. The Los Angeles franchise of the National Basketball Association offered Coach K a five-year, $40 million contract to leave his beloved Blue Devils to coach the Lakers. On the surface, receiving such a lucrative offer appears completely different from being fired, suffering through a major illness, or losing a loved one. And yet, this was perhaps the most significant crucible of his professional career. At the age of 57, receiving such an unexpected and attractive offer forced Coach K to reflect deeply on some very serious questions: What's really important to me? What are my core values? Where do my loyalties lie? What's my real purpose in life? His answer: "I passionately want to coach and teach . . . and your heart has to be in whatever you lead . . . Duke has always taken up my whole heart. And no matter how good some other option was, to lead my Duke team with all my heart could only happen at this place." Coach K remained at Duke. More dedicated than ever, he earned his 1,000th victory in January of 2015, solidifying his position as the coach with most wins in Division I mens' basketball history.

As you scan your life for potential crucibles, be playful. Think broadly. For some, the task of identifying a crucible comes easily. One single, searing moment in their lives seems to define who they are and how they lead. For others, this work can be more difficult, the process more complex, their crucibles more nuanced. Are there any places in your life that you keep revisiting? Events or episodes that seem to hold your attention? These are crucible-rich zip codes, ripe for re-visiting to explore for important lessons.

Many of us can't point to one single, dramatic event that seems worthy of the label. That's okay; don't force it. Relax your criteria. Instead of a single event, your crucible might be an extended period of minor challenges that resulted in an important shift or reframing of yourself or your place in the world. It could also be a series of events over time that reveals an important pattern in your life. Who knows? You might be in the middle of an important crucible right now.

Don't worry if your crucible doesn't seem to fit the formal definition. Don't worry if your life seems largely blessed, if you haven't experienced any dramatic hardships, trauma, or crises worthy of a good novel. This exercise is not about unleashing your competitive juices to see who has lived the most challenging life. It's simply designed to ensure that you squeeze as much learning out of the rock that is your life story. It's as simple (and hard) as that. Let's try it!

POTENTIAL CRUCIBLES

As you scan your life story, what events, relationships, or periods of your life have had the greatest impact on who you are? Start by searching for potential crucibles. For example: My parents divorced when I was eight years old; I was elected president of my high school class; I was passed over for promotion; I was cut from the JV basketball team; my partner of six years just broke up with me; when I was 12, my parents sent me from China to live in the United States with my grandparents and I didn't speak any English; I wasn't very popular in high school or college; one of my children has no respect for me; I have the chance to start my own company, but I also have an offer to return to a prestigious consulting firm; my boss screamed at me in an important meeting with a client; I am in love with a person from outside my faith; I spent three years in financial services and hated it, but loved the money; my father is dying; I just started in my first real leadership position, and I'm not sure that I can do this.

EXERCISE 3.1: POTENTIAL CRUCIBLES

List at least three to five potential crucibles:

- _____
- _____
- _____
- _____
- _____

Your Greatest Crucible. Now, try to identify the single, most salient, and consequential experience of your life. If you had to point to just one life-defining event, which one would it be? Which one of the potential crucibles listed above seems to hold the most meaning for you? Identify your greatest crucible with an **asterisk** next to it (above).

Pattern of Crucibles. If, upon reflection, no one single experience rises to the level of feeling particularly life defining or extraordinarily salient, then look for a pattern of crucibles in your life. Can you identify a significant theme or common thread that seems to flow through your life story, one that seems to define who you are? If you can, how would you describe this pattern?

_____

_____

_____

_____

Multiple Crucibles. For this exercise, it's important to work really hard at identifying a single greatest crucible or discerning a central pattern. Don't give up too easily on either of these drills. After some effort though, if selecting a greatest crucible simply doesn't feel right and no clear pattern emerges, then simply hang onto your original list of potential crucibles. You'll need them for the next part of this exercise.

THE STORY OF YOUR CRUCIBLE

It's time to write the story of your crucible. Whether it's based on a single event, a pattern of experiences, or a list of important stories, the very practice of writing it down—putting it out there—is an essential step in the learning process. You might be thinking, "I can skip this step. I've done the reflection, but writing is hard. Can't I get the benefit of this exercise without having to write it down?" The short answer is, "No."

Reflection is important; however, until we write it down, we don't really get it. The very discipline of writing infuses a level of clarity into our understanding that simply doesn't exist until we get it down on paper. Writing also injects some much-needed space between our experiences and ourselves. Until we write about them, in a sense, our experiences "have us." The very act of writing shifts the locus of agency and control; putting our lives "out there" allows us to "have them." Gaining some distance from our stories, from ourselves, can be very liberating. Writing our stories in this unique format—as crucibles—also allows us to more easily and powerfully share ourselves with others.

EXERCISE 3.2: THE STORY OF YOUR CRUCIBLE(S)

Write a letter to yourself that tells the story of your life's crucible. Write it in one continuous draft, allowing as much space as you need to complete the letter. As you write, tell the whole story, with a beginning, middle, and end. Set the stage, narrate the high point, include all relevant details. We are indeed the authors of own lives. This is a chance to write your story. Not the entire story, but the most salient moment (or moments) of it. Have some fun with this. Write something you will want to read again and again. No matter how potentially painful it might be to relive these important moments, ignoring them is not an option if you want to better understand yourself and make progress on your journey toward authenticity.

Your life's crucible:

_____

_____

_____

_____

_____

_____

_____

_____

_____

_____

_____

_____

_____

_____

_____

_____

_____

_____

LEARNING FROM YOUR CRUCIBLE

Having addressed the first question: What events, relationships, or periods of your life have had the greatest impact on who you are? let's now turn to the second: What did you learn from these crucibles?

At this point, you might be thinking: While it might be an interesting intellectual exercise to identify potential crucibles in my life, what's the point? This is more than a parlor game. The purpose of this entire exercise is to gain greater clarity about who you are, your authentic self, your True North.

Once you've identified your crucible, an important pattern, or a series of crucibles, the next step is to squeeze them for all they're worth. The following questions will help you mine these experiences for as much meaning as possible:

- In general, how do you respond to crucibles in your life?
  - Do you continue to spiral downward or come out stronger?
  - Do you learn anything from these extraordinary moments?
- What do you learn from them?
  - What lessons (about others, the world, business, leadership, etc.) do you take away from your crucible?
  - What do you learn about yourself?

People vary greatly along each of these dimensions. For your continued growth as a leader, it's important to understand how you tend to respond in a crucible. As you review some of the most consequential moments of your life, can you identify a general pattern in how you respond to them?

While not all crucibles involve pain or loss, most involve an internal struggle of some consequence. When faced with particularly searing moments in life, what is your general pattern of response? How you tend to deal with such battles is important to know. Do you tend to ignore them, hoping they'll go away? Or do you seek them out and embrace them as potential learning experiences?

Not all of us are as fortunate as Coach K to have a $40 million offer trigger deep self-reflection. In fact, most crucibles are indeed painful; many involve some form of loss. Adversity gets our attention; difficulties challenge us to our core. When things go well, when the world is largely working for us, we rarely pause to consider alternative ways of knowing, doing, or being.

One way to summarize the two puzzles outlined above is to combine them into one single, deeply important question: How do you respond to adversity? Fortunately, there is a large body of research to help us address this question. If you are interested in learning more, there are dozens of good books on resilience, hardiness, and grit. We've listed a few at the end of this chapter.

Happily we don't need to understand the science to learn from our experiences. In fact, we think you'll find the research more useful if you first work hard at unpacking your own crucibles. Here are some questions to help you do this important work:

EXERCISE 3.3: LEARNING FROM YOUR CRUCIBLE

Review the letter you just wrote describing your life's crucible. What did you learn from it?

What lessons (about the world, business, leadership, etc.) did you take away from this experience?

What did you learn about yourself?

_____

_____

_____

_____

_____

_____

_____

_____

_____

_____

_____

_____

In general, how do you tend to respond to adversity?

_____

_____

_____

_____

_____

_____

_____

_____

_____

_____

_____

_____

What resources did you call upon to help get through this crucible?

_____

_____

_____

_____

_____

_____

_____

_____

_____

_____

Our lives are chock-full of potential developmental experiences. Not all of them rise to the significance of a crucible. However, the general process of identifying, reflecting, and learning from them is largely the same as the one you've practiced here. In Part Two, "Discover Your Authentic Leadership," you'll apply this same discipline to increase your level of self-awareness in several critical areas of development.

KEY TAKEAWAYS

- There are a few particularly salient events, relationships, or periods in our lives that have a disproportionate impact on who we are and how we lead. We call these crucibles.

- Identifying, reflecting, and writing about these experiences is an important process in discovering our True North.

- Understanding how we respond to life's crucibles is important to understanding how we grow and develop.

SUGGESTED READING

Bennis, W., and Thomas, R. *Geeks and Geezers*. Boston: Harvard Business School Press, 2002.

Coelho, P. *The Alchemist*. New York: HarperCollins, 2006.

Maddi, S. R. *Hardiness: Turning Stressful Circumstances into Resilient Growth*. Heidelberg: Springer, 2013.

Quinn, R. E. *Building the Bridge as You Walk on It: A Guide for Leading Change*. San Francisco: Jossey-Bass, 2004.

Reivich, K. Shatté A. *The Resilience Factor*. New York: Broadway Books, 2002.

Seligman, M. E. P. *Learned Optimism*. New York: Random House, 2006.

Stolz, P. *Grit: The New Science of What it Takes to Persevere, Flourish, Succeed*. New York: Climb Strong Press, 2015.

Thomas, R. *Crucibles of Leadership: How to Learn from Experience to Become a Great Leader*. Boston: Harvard Business School Press, 2008.

Part Two

Discover Your
Authentic Leadership

> Follow your compass and not your clock.
> —*Ann Moore, CEO, Time, Inc.*

To find your way in the wilderness, you need both a map and a compass. In Part One, we asked you to sketch out the broad terrain of your journey by charting your life story. You now have a rough map that includes potential hazards for losing your way, as well as some of the most important peaks and valleys as defined by your crucibles.

In *Discover Your True North*, we share stories that reveal some of the challenges leaders faced when trying to remain aligned with their True North—their most deeply held beliefs, values, and principles. As you face similar pressures and seductions of leading in the real world, you not only need an accurate map, but also a solid compass to help you gain and maintain your bearings along the way. Part Two provides that compass.

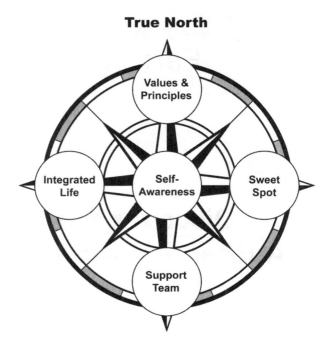

A Compass for the Journey

At the center lies "self-awareness"—the capacity for introspection and ability to see oneself clearly. Everything turns on this; your journey toward becoming an authentic leader begins and ends here. Represented by each of the cardinal directions are four critical areas of development: practice your values, find your sweet spot, build your support team, and integrate your life. These four developmental mandates emerged out of our interviews with authentic leaders as significant signposts pointing the way toward True North.

Discovering and following these mandates is hard work. There are no shortcuts here, no quick fixes, no "becoming an authentic leader in seven easy steps." To become an authentic leader, first you must take responsibility for your own development and then use this compass to guide your journey.

As you complete the exercises in Part Two, you will find that all five parts of the compass fit together as an integrated whole. To consistently live your True North requires paying attention to all five. Development in each of these areas is a lifelong journey. We are never completely self-aware; we can always live more aligned with our values;

discovering new sweet spots is one of the great mysteries of life; a healthy support team requires constant nourishment and attention; and the secret to living an integrated life is understanding that you are never done!

You are embarking on an exciting journey to discover your authentic leadership. Let's get started.

4

Develop Your Self-Awareness

> I have often thought that the best way to define a man's character would be to seek out the particular mental or moral attitude in which, when it came upon him, he felt himself most deeply and intensively active and alive. At such moments, there is a voice inside which speaks and says, "This is the real me."
> —*William James*, Letters of William James

We have placed self-awareness at the center of the True North compass because everything turns on it. A compass needle orients itself to Earth's magnetic field. To do so, it pivots on the fixed point of a tiny fulcrum. Self-awareness is the pivot point upon which all development depends. Without self-awareness there is nothing to anchor your journey, no way to orient yourself, no way of knowing if you are losing or finding your way. Discovering your True North requires a willingness to be vulnerable and a capacity for honest introspection—a lifelong commitment to become more self-aware.

So how self-aware are you? When you look in the mirror, how clear is the picture? How well do you really know yourself? How comfortable are you with yourself? How accepting are you of that person in the mirror? Progress on your journey toward becoming a more authentic leader is marked by how you answer these fundamental questions. At some deep level, this entire fieldbook is designed to help you gain greater clarity about who you are, your values, motivations, strengths and weaknesses—your purpose.

This chapter goes straight at these issues. Becoming more self-aware takes work. It is a discipline that can be learned; but like most habits, it requires real commitment and more than a little courage to develop. Therefore, when completing the exercises in this chapter, be as open and honest as you can. The potential rewards are great. To paraphrase William James, when was the last time you felt "most deeply and intensively active and alive"? When was the last time you heard that "voice inside" say "this is the real me"? How wonderful would it be to hear that voice more often? It's possible, so let's get started.

SELF-AWARENESS CAN BE DEVELOPED

It's been 20 years since Daniel Goleman wrote his groundbreaking book, *Emotional Intelligence (EQ)*. There are five dimensions to EQ: self-awareness, self-regulation, empathy, motivation, and social skills. Unlike IQ, research has shown that it is possible to make significant improvements in our emotional intelligence. In this chapter we'll focus on the first three, starting and ending with self-awareness. In Chapter 6, we'll examine motivation, and in Chapters 7, 8, and 11, we'll address social skills from multiple angles.

EXERCISE 4.1: ASSESSING YOUR EQ

In 1902, sociologist Charles Cooley coined the phrase "looking-glass self" to emphasize the importance others' perceptions have on our own views of ourselves. Cooley's insight is boiled down to this one famous phrase attributed to him, "I am not what I think I am; I am not what you think I am; I am what I think you think I am." That picture we see in the mirror each morning is likely not exactly the same as the one our parents see, which is likely different from the one our friends see. Much of what we know about ourselves comes from how we see ourselves through the eyes of others.

If you truly want to become more self-aware, then you have to enlist the aid of others. You cannot do this work alone. As you'll see, we recommend that you ask at least five people to help you complete the next set of exercises. The more people you engage, the more complete the picture of yourself. This is not only true for this exercise, but for your life!

The following questions encourage you to compare a personal evaluation of yourself with how others see you. For those questions requiring a numerical evaluation, rate yourself on a scale of 1–5 (with 1 meaning "to the *least* extent or degree," 3 meaning "to a *moderate* extent or degree," and 5 meaning "to the *greatest* extent or degree"), then support your assessment by answering each question. Complete your own assessments before incorporating feedback from others.

I. Self-Awareness

Self-awareness: the ability to see yourself clearly, to recognize and understand your moods, emotions, and drives as well as the impact you have on others.

	Self-Rating (1–5)	Rating from Others (1–5)
How self-confident am I?		
How self-accepting am I?		
How comfortable am I with who I am?		
How aware am I of my moods, my emotions, and my drives?		
How aware am I of the impact I have on other people?		

Describe a situation in which you demonstrated a lack of self-awareness.

_____

_____

_____

In what contexts or situations do you tend to exhibit low self-awareness?

_____

_____

_____

What steps can you take to improve your self-awareness?

1. _____
2. _____
3. _____
4. _____
5. _____

Overall assessment of your self-awareness (1–5): _____   _____

                                         Self   *Others*

II. Self-Regulation

Self-regulation: the ability to control or redirect disruptive impulses and moods; the ability to act in your long-term best interest consistent with your core values; the ability to suspend judgment and think before acting.

	Self-Rating (1–5)	Rating from Others (1–5)
How effective am I at regulating my moods so as to minimize their impact on other people?		
To what extent am I able to suspend judgment of others and their ideas, in order to gain a full understanding first?		
When confronted with situations that disappoint or anger me, to what extent am I able to pause, disengage, and think clearly before responding or reacting?		
When I receive critical feedback, how well am I able to actually "hear it" and respond in a constructive manner without getting defensive or attacking the source?		
To what extent am I comfortable in novel situations?		
To what extent am I comfortable responding to ambiguity and change?		

Describe a situation in which you demonstrated a lack of self-regulation.

_____

_____

_____

In what contexts or situations do you struggle most with self-regulation?

_____

_____

_____

What steps can you take to improve your ability to more consistently self-regulate?

1. _____

2. _____

3. _____

4. _____

5. _____

Overall assessment of your self-regulation (1–5): _____ _____

                                                                    Self   *Others*

III. Empathy

Empathy: the ability to understand and be sensitive to other's emotions and experience a situation from their frame of reference.

	Self-Rating (1–5)	Rating from Others (1–5)
How good am I at understanding another's perspective or experience?		
How well do I understand the emotions of others?		
How likely am I to respond in a sensitive and helpful way to others' emotional needs?		
To what extent do others view me as sensitive and empathic?		

Describe a situation in which you demonstrated a lack of empathy for others.

_____

_____

_____

In what settings or under what conditions do you find it most difficult to demonstrate empathy?

_____

_____

_____

What steps should you take to be more empathic?

1. _____
2. _____
3. _____
4. _____
5. _____

Overall assessment of empathy (1–5):   _____   _____
                                                      Self   *Others*

Truly seeing ourselves as others see us can be difficult. As you review others' assessments, you are likely to find that some of their perspectives differ from yours. Such differences should be expected and represent a potentially powerful learning opportunity. First, monitor your emotional response to reading their assessments. How open are you to hearing what they have to say? How defensive are you? How will you incorporate their perspective into your own?

When it comes to self-awareness, self-regulation, and empathy, the looking-glass self can sometimes feel more like a house of mirrors. When truly seeing yourself through the eyes of others, what do you see? A cartoon-like caricature, full of unrecognizable distortions? Or an increasingly refined, more complex sense of who you truly are? The important question is not, "Who is right?" The real question is, "What will you do with this new information?" Incorporate it into your ever-evolving sense of self, or dismiss it and cling to your own self-serving, less accurate portrayal?

DISCOVERING YOUR AUTHENTIC SELF

It is impossible to be authentic without being aware of your core strengths and weaknesses. You also need to identify and understand your blind spots, hot buttons, and areas of vulnerability.

We all know people who represent themselves in one way and then behave in exactly the opposite. In reality, you may have been guilty of this as well. This is a working definition of being inauthentic. Authenticity is not about being perfect, either. People who behave as if they are perfect are just as inauthentic.

As we have seen from our research, those leaders who can speak openly about their weaknesses, blind spots, and vulnerabilities permit others to do the same. If you can do this, you will create deep levels of trust and commitment. You will be living with the humble truth of owning and accepting *all* of who you are, your gifts as well as your weaknesses.

We each have many aspects that we present to the world in layered succession. In *Discover Your True North*, we introduced the metaphor of an onion with all its layers.

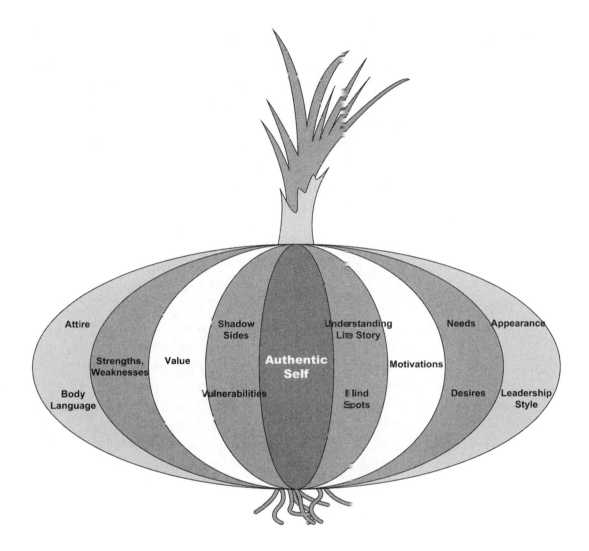

Outer layers are expressions of our external identity to the world. These are the first signals to other people about who we are and what lies beneath. Yet they are also forms of protection; they prevent the world from seeing our deeper selves. Underneath the surface skin lie deeper layers: our strengths and weaknesses, our needs and desires. These elements shape and drive what others see on the surface. Deeper still lie our values and motivations, criteria that define our sense of success and fulfillment in the world.

Most hidden of all are our shadow sides, our vulnerabilities, and our blind spots. We all have them, whether we are aware of them or willing to acknowledge them or not. Either way, these deeper layers powerfully influence who we are, yet by their very nature they are hard to see. Unless we are brutally honest with ourselves or invite others to give us candid feedback, these important forces remain hidden and influence us in ways both potent and unpredictable.

At the very core of our being lies our authentic self—our true and genuine nature, our identity. If we can "own" all aspects of who we are, we can live in harmony with our authentic selves and present our true selves with confidence and comfort to the world. Our True North comes from this authentic place, from which springs our calling, our purpose.

Why is the outer skin of our onion so tough? For fear of being judged harshly by others, or possibly rejected, we are reluctant to expose our deeper layers. We want to display our strengths, but work hard to hide any weakness.

As a result of such fears, we try to hide our deeper selves, where our vulnerabilities, weaknesses, blind spots, and shadow sides reside. Many of us are so good at covering them up that we ourselves are not aware of them, yet others see them so clearly. Frequently, we remain in denial until powerful forces or situations reveal them to the world, often with unfortunate consequences. When leading, being forced into a situation where parts of ourselves are suddenly exposed can often result in us losing our way.

The paradox underlying this process of revealing only parts of ourselves while hiding others is that our vulnerabilities, shadow sides, and blind spots are also the parts of us most starved for expression, acceptance, and integration. When we fail to acknowledge them as being just as central to our identities as our strengths, they cause us to behave in inauthentic ways. Only when we embrace these largely hidden aspects of ourselves can we become fully authentic as human beings.

SELF-ACCEPTANCE

The good news about self-awareness is that it can lead you to accept yourself as you really are. It is a simple fact that none of us can be the best at everything. Each of us has a set of strengths that come naturally, talents we have developed over time, and things we are never going to be good at. At the same time, what enables us to be authentic is maximizing the use of our strengths—not focusing on our weaknesses—and surrounding ourselves with others whose strengths complement our own and fill in for our gaps. The ability to accept ourselves as we are is a gift that leads not only to self-acceptance, but to true freedom.

We have found that accepting yourself for who you are and loving yourself unconditionally requires compassion. In order to acknowledge your weaknesses and shadow sides, you have to accept the things you like least about yourself as being integral to who you are. We see this illustrated in the following reflection when Bill learned to accept his weaknesses:

In 1997 when I was chairman and CEO of Medtronic, I was driving from downtown Minneapolis to my office listening to a CD featuring an address by poet David Whyte called "The Poetry of Self-Compassion." One of the poems recited by Whyte was "Love After Love" [see sidebar], by the Nobel Prize–winning poet Derek Walcott. Walcott's poem talks about the challenge of getting in touch with those parts of ourselves that we have rejected, denied, and ignored for many years. Walcott encourages us to "invite them into the feast that is our life."

I was so stunned by these words as I listened to Whyte recite the poem that I pulled my car over to the shoulder of I-94 several times in order to write them down. In retrospect, this seems pretty silly, as this was just a CD and I could have easily written down the poem after I arrived at my office.

Love After Love
DEREK WALCOTT

The time will come when, with elation,
You will greet yourself arriving at your own door,
In your own mirror, and each will smile at the other's welcome,
And say, sit here. Eat.
You will love again the stranger who was yourself.
Give wine. Give bread. Give back your heart to itself,
To the stranger who has loved you all your life,
Whom you ignored for another,
Who knows you by heart.
Take down the love letters from the bookshelf,
The photographs, the desperate notes,
Peel your own image from the mirror.
Sit. Feast on your life.

Why was I so stunned by these words? I was moved because I had been trying so hard to be perfect all my life that I had rejected my shadow sides and my vulnerabilities for more than 40 years. In that moment, I finally recognized that I had been rejecting parts of myself that I did not like and had tried unsuccessfully to hide from others. These included my impatience, direct manner of challenging others, and often aggressive behavior, coupled with a long-ago memory of being a skinny kid who was picked on by bigger kids in junior high. Even worse, I had been blaming these characteristics on my then-deceased father, who had similar traits, instead of accepting them as integral to who I am. This poem finally enabled me to accept myself with all my warts. Once I did so, I found I could love all of myself, not just the good parts, and become much more authentic in my relationships with others. Even more important, accepting myself for who I was, flaws and all, became very liberating for me.

EXERCISE 4.2: PEELING BACK THE ONION

The purpose of this exercise is to help you become more accepting by first acknowledging some of those areas you are least proud of.

What are your "shadow sides," those aspects of yourself that you are least proud, those features or traits you know about but don't like to acknowledge, areas where you feel particularly vulnerable to exposure?

1. _____
2. _____
3. _____
4. _____
5. _____

Many leaders find that their strengths are actually closely related to their vulnerabilities and weaknesses. Although some parts of who we are might be hard to accept, when we see them as an integral part of who we are, just as we see those parts of which we are most proud, we just might find that it is easier to accept ourselves with all our strengths and weaknesses. After all, they are simply two sides of the same coin. Our weaknesses are just as much a part of who we are as are our strengths. Developing a healthy relationship with both of them is essential to becoming more self-accepting and ultimately more comfortable with who we really are, not that over-the-top, lopsided, résumé version we work so hard to present to the world every day.

FEEDBACK SEEKING

Seeking feedback is the single most effective way to increase self-awareness. We all have personal blind spots, certain aspects of ourselves that we can't see but others can. It is only through others that we learn about these blind spots and see ourselves as we truly are, and not just as we think we are.

Good friends call you out when you're not being yourself, when you're trying too hard, when you're being inauthentic. Really good friends are those who not only see your blinds spots, but who also have the courage to share them with you in a way that you can truly hear it.

Personal blind spots are areas that are visible to others—sometimes painfully so—but not to you. The developmental challenge of blind spots is that you don't know what you don't know. And yet, what you don't know can still hurt you. Like that area in the side mirror of your car where you can't see that truck in the lane next to you, personal blind spots can easily be overlooked because you are completely unaware of their presence. They can be equally dangerous as well. That truck you don't see? It's really there! So are your blind spots. Just because you don't see them, doesn't mean they can't run you over.

This is where you need to enlist the help of others—not critics, but people you trust. You have to develop a crew of these special people, people who are willing to hold up that mirror, who not only know you well enough to see that truck, but who also care enough about you to let you know that it's there. Of course the challenge is not only finding these kinds of friends; the real trick is keeping them. How you ask for and respond to this type of difficult feedback will determine whether or not you have enough of these people in your life. We'll go straight at this challenge in Chapter 7: Build Your Support Team.

EXERCISE 4.3: GETTING HONEST FEEDBACK FROM OTHERS

The purpose of this exercise is to explore your ability to ask for and receive honest feedback. Unfortunately, good, honest feedback is often hard to come by. If you are like most of us, you're not very good at asking for it. How many people do you have in your life whom you can easily approach, ask for frank input, receive some, and actually hear it?

List the names of those people in your life that you can count on for good, honest, frank feedback:

_____

_____

_____

How long is your list? Hang onto this insight. It's the starting point for that deeper conversation we'll have about support teams in Chapter 7.

Most of us don't *really* want honest feedback simply because, when it's really good, it's often painful to hear. All of us crave positive feedback. As high-need-for-achievement people, many of us can't live without feedback; we need constant attention and reinforcement from others. However, few of us have the courage to surround ourselves with people who are willing to call us out when we are slipping; even fewer still have the courage to live our lives as disciplined feedback-seekers.

When was the last time you received some honest feedback that was perhaps a bit difficult to hear? What was it about the situation or relationship that generated such feedback?

_____

_____

_____

_____

_____

What was the feedback? How did you react to it? What were your feelings about it and the person who offered it?

_____

_____

_____

_____

_____

_____

Did you learn anything from this situation or feedback? If so, what did you learn and what changes, if any, have you made as a result of receiving this "gift"?

_____

_____

_____

_____

_____

_____

Are you prepared to share your perceived strengths, weaknesses, vulnerabilities, and shadow sides with someone you feel very close to? If so, we suggest that you seek them out at your earliest opportunity and solicit their feedback by asking them the following question:

"How do you experience me?"

Record what you learned below.

_____

_____

_____

_____

_____

_____

_____

_____

_____

When you received this feedback, there is a good chance that some of it might have surprised you. If it did, these surprises—aspects of yourself that someone else sees but you don't—point to potentially important blind spots. Don't lose sight of them. This is what the journey toward self-awareness is all about: seeking difficult feedback from as many different sources as possible and incorporating these blind spots into your constantly evolving, ever-clearer picture of yourself.

What are your blind spots?

1. _____
2. _____
3. _____
4. _____
5. _____

LEARNING ABOUT YOURSELF IS AN ONGOING PROCESS

In our research, we learned that authentic leaders are always asking for honest feedback from others in order to calibrate their view of themselves. To incorporate such feedback into their behaviors, they then develop regular practices for reflection and introspection. We heard from many of our interviewees that journaling, meditation, spiritual work, and physical exercise—all practices associated with reflection and introspection—were disciplines widely practiced for gaining deeper self-awareness.

There are two keys to making these practices effective in gaining self-awareness and self-acceptance. The first is to be completely honest with yourself as well as with at least one other person in your life. The second is to develop regular habits and build time for introspection into your daily routine.

The goal of self-awareness is self-knowledge and ultimately self-acceptance—self-acceptance as the person you are as well as the one you are capable of becoming.

EXERCISE 4.4: TAKEAWAYS ON SELF-AWARENESS AND SELF-ACCEPTANCE

The purpose of this exercise is to summarize all of the important self-work you've done in one place, to take stock of where you are at this point in your journey toward greater self-awareness and self-acceptance.

Based on all the work you've done to this point, list your top five areas for improvement:

1. _____
2. _____
3. _____
4. _____
5. _____

What are some concrete ways you can become more self-aware?

1. _____
2. _____
3. _____
4. _____
5. _____

How comfortable are you with yourself? What can you do to become more self-accepting?

_____
_____
_____
_____
_____
_____

SELF-AWARENESS IS PREPARATION FOR GROWTH

In this chapter, we introduced the foundation for authenticity: self-awareness. Emotionally intelligent, authentic leaders know themselves. They are not only self-aware, but also self-accepting, comfortable in their own skins. Authentic leaders have a healthy relationship with their strengths and their weaknesses. When they look in the mirror, they see all layers of the onion, understand how each contributes to their uniqueness, and leverage this self-knowledge as the basis for continued growth.

One of the most important dimensions of self-knowledge is our core values—what we care about most, those central beliefs that both define and animate our very being. In the next chapter, we'll help you identify these core values, a central signpost on the path toward True North.

KEY TAKEAWAYS

- Discovering our True North requires a willingness to be vulnerable and a capacity for honest introspection.
- Three ways to improve our emotional intelligence (EQ) are to work on self-awareness, self-regulation, and empathy.
- Like an onion, we have many layers. The outer skin protects us, but it also prevents us from showing our authentic self and rarely fools anyone except ourselves.
- We cannot do this work alone.
- Asking for and receiving meaningful feedback is the only way to identify and eliminate potentially dangerous blind spots.
- Self-awareness is a necessary first step toward self-acceptance.
- The process of becoming more self-aware and self-accepting is a lifelong journey.

SUGGESTED READING

Bennis, W., and Tichy, N. *Judgment*. New York: Portfolio, 2007.

Bryant, J. *Love Leadership: The New Way to Live in a Fear-Based World*. San Francisco: Jossey-Bass, 2009.

Cashman, K. *Leadership from the Inside Out*. Provo, Utah: Executive Excellence, 1998.

Conley, C. *Peak*. San Francisco: Jossey-Bass, 2007.

Cooley, C. H. *Human Nature and the Social Order*. New York: Scribner's, 1902.

Dweck, C. S. *Mindset: The New Psychology of Success*. New York: Random House, 2008.

Gardner, H. *Intelligence Reframed*. New York: Basic Books, 1999.

Gladwell, M. *Blink*. New York: Little, Brown, 2000.

Goldsmith, M. *What Got You Here Won't Get You There*. New York: Hyperion, 2007.

Goleman, D. *Emotional Intelligence*. New York: Bantam Books, 1995.

Goleman, D., Boyatzis, R., and McKee, A. *Primal Leadership*. Boston: Harvard Business School Press, 2002.

Jaworski, J. *Synchronicity*. San Francisco: Berrett-Koehler, 1996.

Langer, E. J. *Mindfulness*. Boston: Da Capo Press, 1983.

Kabat-Zinn, J. *Mindfulness for Beginners*. Boulder: Sounds True, 2012.

Maxwell, J. *Developing the Leader Within You*. London: Nelson, 2005.

Oliver, M. *New and Selected Poems*. Boston: Beacon Press, 1992.

Tan, C. M. *Search Inside Yourself*. New York: Harper Collins, 2012.

Walcott, D. "Love After Love." In *Sea Grapes*. New York: Farrar, Straus & Giroux, 1976.

5

Practice Your Values

We increase integrity by constantly monitoring our lack of integrity.
We are all hypocrites. We all have values we do not live. We refuse to
see our hypocrisy. Yet seeing our hypocrisy is the potential motor
for change. There is so much pain we are willing to close our
integrity gaps. Then we exercise the courage to change.
Instead of fearing uncertainty, we welcome it . . .

—*Bill Tolbert*

It is important to be clear about your authentic values, leadership principles, and ethical boundaries so that you can put them into practice when leading. Living your values enables you to make sound decisions and, more important, enables others to trust you. In looking critically at your actions under pressure, you will learn from times when you lived by your values, and from those times when you deviated from them.

In this chapter, you will identify your core values. Next, you will translate those values into their associated leadership principles (values in practice). Finally, you will define the ethical boundaries beyond which you will not go.

VALUES ARE PERSONAL

We are deeply shaped by our values and how well we live them. Practicing your values in a consistent way brings meaning to your work and life, and enables you to be congruent and authentic. Others' trust of you is deeply impacted by how predictable you are in living your values, especially when the chips are down. These moments are what others remember and what one celebrates years later when the hard right is chosen over the easy wrong.

Thus, whenever you lead in any context, your actions are being watched as you demonstrate your values in what you do. People around you are looking not only at the effectiveness of your actions but also at the way you act and the choices you make. Securing trust when it has been lost by those who came before you, as well as restoring it when it is strained by our own actions, is among the most difficult and important challenges that we all face.

Although not all values are shared by all leaders, we believe integrity is a value that's required for one to be an authentic leader. Per the quote at the beginning of the chapter, really living any core value means we must be willing to see where we are not living it and then close the gap to reach the next level of mastery.

IDENTIFYING VALUES, PRINCIPLES, AND ETHICAL BOUNDARIES

To operate from your True North, you not only need to know what they are, but also how to translate them into practice. Those who develop a clear sense of their values, principles, and ethical boundaries before they find themselves in the midst of a crisis are better prepared to navigate through difficult decisions and dilemmas when the pressure is on.

EXERCISE 5.1: IDENTIFYING YOUR VALUES

Core Value: an ideal that you care so deeply about that it is integral to your life.

The purpose of this exercise is to identify the core values that define your leadership.

Part I. Discovering Your Core Values

We are looking for the core values that are central to who you are and will define you as a leader. We are not looking for values that you aspire to living or ones that you like. We want to discover the values that are integral to who you are no matter the circumstances. One place to find these core values is to look through the lens of your crucible stories. We want to find the core values you ignored that contributed to the severity of your crucible stories or the ones that got you back home after you lost your way. These core values are your teachers that, over time, reveal who you are in both good and bad times.

Return to Exercise 3.2, "The Story of Your Crucible(s)," to complete the following questions

As you consider your crucible(s), which values contributed to the crucible occurring—or its severity—because you ignored them, put them aside at some point, or because you just weren't aware they were important? (See list of values at the end of the chapter for examples, and feel free to be creative.)

1. _____

2. _____

3. _____

4. _____

5. _____

What were the values that got you through your crucible?

1. _____

2. _____

3. _____

4. _____

5. _____

How are these core values demonstrated in the stories you wrote that described your proudest leadership experiences? (See Exercise 1.2)

1. _____

2. _____

3. _____

4. _____

5. _____

Part II. Your Core Values

Now tighten up the list you created in Part I by listing only the values that are *most* important to your life and who you are as an authentic leader.

The following 1–6 are the core values that define your leadership:

1. _____   4. _____

2. _____   5. _____

3. _____   6. _____

Describe actions/situations in which you displayed your top 3 core values:

Core Value 1: _____

Action/Situation: _____

_____

_____

Core Value 2: _____

Action/Situation: _____

_____

_____

Core Value 3: _____

Action/Situation: _____

_____

_____

Part III. Clarifying Your Core Values

One of the key challenges when leading others is that it's not enough to simply state your core values: integrity, honesty, respect for others, etc. Our cultural background and life journey significantly impacts the meaning we associate with a given value. How you

Table 5.1: Definitions of Your Values

Value Name	Value Definition

define the value at this time and place in your life is more important. Your definition may not match anyone else's, and that's okay.

Below is an example of very different definitions of *integrity* that were created by individuals in our programs. Each one grew up and operated under very different cultural norms, which greatly impacted their definitions.

Integrity: Tell the whole truth to others and operate within the law in all business concerns.

Integrity: Make sure all my family and extended family members equally benefit from my success in their access to work opportunities within my business as well as financial wealth.

It would be hard to image two more different definitions. This is why it's so important to create authentic definitions of *your* core values that are true for you.

Take the three core values you defined in Part II and place them in Table 5.1. Use the action/situation you described to help create a powerful and clear definition of each value.

Part IV. Living Your Values in Challenging Times

When things are going well, it is relatively easy to practice one's values in a consistent manner. The real test comes when things are not going your way or when you can see years of success being threatened. What will you do then? Everyone watches to see what you will do under pressure, when you are feeling the heat in the crucible. Will you deviate—just a little bit—in order to get through this crisis, thinking that you will return to your values once it passes? If you do, others around you will no longer see you as someone who "walks the talk." Observing your example, others may assume that they too can deviate from their values under pressure.

Even though you may go back to practicing your values when the pressure eases, the next time you find yourself in a similar challenging situation, you may be tempted to deviate again—especially if you got away with it the first time.

An even more critical test is what you will do when you do have power and you are finally in charge of the cookie jar!

> Nearly all men can stand adversity, but if you want to test a man's character, give him power.
>
> —Abraham Lincoln

We find that this is precisely the way that many leaders get in trouble: They think they won't get caught.

Can you look yourself in the mirror and say that you have stayed true to your values in challenging circumstances? Or would you admit to yourself that you have not?

_____

_____

_____

_____

Looking back over your life story, describe a situation in which you deviated from your core values in order to achieve your goals.

_____

_____

_____

_____

How can you better handle this situation if you face it in the future (who could you enroll in helping you stay true to yourself)?

_____

_____

_____

_____

Many people get on a slippery slope with regard to their values as minor deviations lead to major ones later on.

Is there a predictable pattern where these relatively minor transgressions can/have built into something larger?

_____

_____

_____

How can you sense when you are heading down this slippery slope?

_____

_____

_____

Part VI. Exploring Conflicts among Your Values

Some of our most challenging moments occur not when we are faced with violating our core values; rather, they appear when two core values are in conflict.

A basic conflict most of us face is when we have a strong friendship with someone whose skills are not up to the task. The value of the relationship is in conflict with the value of getting an "A" on the project. Do we just work harder to make up for their lack of skill, or do we replace them with someone who is more skilled?

Real authentic leadership is defined by how we handle these moments in our lives.

Reviewing your life story once again, describe a situation in which at least two of your core values conflicted with each other.

_____

_____

_____

How did you resolve this conflict?

_____

_____

_____

Were you pleased with the outcome? How might you handle it differently in the future?

_____

_____

_____

LEADERSHIP PRINCIPLES: MAKING YOUR VALUES ACTIONABLE

As you can see from the work so far in this chapter, living our core values 100 percent of the time is a journey, not a destination. We are always "closing the gap" or seeing where we could move even more fully toward a way to further honor our core values. To do this we must identify a set of practices as well as a way of getting accurate feedback, just like in any other area we wish to master. Visible leadership roles only increase the challenge because:

A. Under intense pressure—in the loneliness of leadership—the only values you can count on are those that you have already tested and proven during your life.

B. In a global world in which values such as integrity or trust have dramatically different meanings, it's how you live your values—not what you say—that matters most.

C.   With the level of 24/7 transparency in today's world, any level of misalignment between your words and deeds will significantly devalue your image.

Thus, a key process to increase the likelihood that we'll live our values when they really matter is to define measurable working practices that allow others to experience us as truly values-based leaders. But we can't do this alone. Yes, there is the myth that we should be strong enough to do it alone, but it is just that: a myth.

In the complex global world we live in, we need others to provide us with accurate feedback to maximize our alignment of words and deeds. Our leadership principles are the linchpins that link our values to the True North of our leadership.

EXERCISE 5.2: IDENTIFYING YOUR LEADERSHIP PRINCIPLES (VALUES IN PRACTICE)

Leadership Principles: Working practices that clarify how you live your values and are measurable in ways that allow you to get helpful feedback and support.

The good news for most us is that 90–95 percent of the time we find it easy to operate from our core values. The purpose of this exercise is to help you define those leadership principles (working practices) that will help you navigate through the challenging times when it's more difficult to live from your core values (the other 5–10 percent of the time).

Use the following two questions as guides:

- What situation(s) are you in where your core values are most tested (the 10 percent of the time that you find it hardest to live those values)?
- How will you solicit feedback about those situations that is accurate and supportive?

Here is an example of a value definition translated into a leadership principle for coauthor Nick Craig:

Truth is one of my core values. I have found in my life that when the truth is about helping someone else see the deeper story or embracing/sharing an article with counterintuitive insights, it is very easy to live my definition of truth. I also have done a great deal of self-reflection, which has uncovered many deep truths about myself.

It is when I am operating in a formal leadership role that my willingness to uncover the deeper truth about how I am doing is compromised. Because my own level of self-criticism is so high, I tend to resist anyone else's input. This is the place I realized I had to create a leadership principle if truth really was a core value for me.

Nick's definition of Truth: The deeper and more powerful insight that lies beneath the surface story.

Nick's Leadership Principle for Truth: Regularly welcome the truth about how others experience me as a leader.

By adhering to the following practices:

- *Monthly:* Hold a one-hour check-in with John (has known me for 15 years and has no problem telling me as it is!) to review how others on the staff are experiencing me in key meetings.
- *Annually:* Have an independent resource interview all of the facilitators we use to deliver our programs, as well as all of our key clients, to give feedback on the organization as well as my leadership.

"The reality is that as much as I love teaching programs on leadership, I sometimes don't see myself as a leader. However, significant feedback indicates that others do see me as a leader, I now have to own that. I think for most of us, others see us as leaders in far more situations than we experience ourselves as leading.

Having applied the above procedures for the past two years, I have discovered that the hardest feedback to hear has been what I am doing well. But I have also gagged at times to learn about the gap between how I thought I was showing up versus reality. Having a monthly checkup has allowed me to address these issues in a time frame that works.

Notice that the above example involves the collaboration of others on my journey. This is a critical element to exploring how to live one's values. Also note how measurable these examples are, in terms of whether Nick did them or not.

Let's now take your top three core values and create powerful leadership principles:

Core Value 1:

What situation(s) are you in where your use of your core value is tested (the 10 percent that's hardest to pull off)?

_____

_____

_____

What leadership principle will help you better honor your core value in those difficult situations?

_____

_____

_____

How will you put into place a means of getting effective and regular feedback from others on how well you are living your core value in these difficult situations?

_____

_____

_____

Core Value 2:

What situation(s) are you in where your use of your core value is tested (the 10 percent that's hardest to pull off)?

_____

_____

_____

What leadership principle will help you better honor your core value in those difficult situations?

_____

_____

_____

How will you put into place a means of getting effective and regular feedback from others on how well you are living your core value in these difficult situations?

_____

_____

_____

Core Value 3:

What situation(s) are you in where your use of your core value is tested (the 10 percent that's hardest to pull off)?

_____

_____

_____

What leadership principle will help you better honor your core value in those difficult situations?

_____

_____

_____

How will you put into place a means of getting effective and regular feedback from others on how well you are living your core value in these difficult situations?

_____

_____

_____

ESTABLISHING ETHICAL BOUNDARIES

Injustice anywhere is a threat to justice everywhere.
We are caught in an inescapable network of mutuality, tied
in a single garment of destiny.
Whatever affects one directly, affects all indirectly.

Martin Luther King
Birmingham jail

Explicit ethical boundaries are the final line of defense against losing sight of your True North. There may be times when you face conflicts among your values that force you to choose one over another, or when you cannot put your leadership principles into practice. It's during these moments when your ethical boundaries represent the clear line in the sand that you will not cross, no matter what.

For example, in Bill's work at Medtronic, the practice of taking a physician out to dinner, going to a ball game, or having an educational meeting at an attractive resort might fall into the "gray area" of values, yet still be considered ethical. In contrast, giving any cash gift or gratuity to a customer anywhere in the world would violate his ethical boundaries and those of the company. Deviations from this boundary would be cause for immediate dismissal of an employee, no matter how valuable that person might be to the organization.

Some leaders have shared with us the practice of writing down their ethical boundaries on a small card that they then carry in their purse, wallet, briefcase, or carry-on. Once you have made such a list, it is a valuable exercise to review it periodically and give yourself a frank self-assessment about whether those boundaries are being tested—are their limits being stretched?—and whether the boundaries are sufficient.

Without such clear ethical boundaries, leaders may find that small deviations early on lead to larger ones later, especially if the earlier deviations are not detected. By this point leaders may discover that they operating are far outside their ethical standards with no way to get back inside. Unless they have the courage to admit to these ethical deviations, leaders may attempt to cover them up. That cover-up often leads to far greater consequences than the original ethical deviation itself.

Much preferred is for leaders to establish their ethical boundaries *before* those boundaries are tested under the inevitable pressures and seductions of the real world.

EXERCISE 5.3: IDENTIFYING YOUR ETHICAL BOUNDARIES

Ethical boundaries: Clear, concrete limits placed on your actions, consistent with your core values.

The purpose of this exercise is to identify and define ethical boundaries for your leadership.

I will always . . .	*I will never . . .*
1.	1.
2.	2.
3.	3.
4.	4.
5.	5.

Looking at your life story, describe a situation in which your ethical boundaries were tested.

_____

_____

_____

How did you respond?

_____

_____

_____

What will you do differently if you are confronted with a similar situation in the future?

_____

_____

_____

The Newspaper Test of Your Ethical Boundaries

Imagine that a challenging action from your work or home life that you are about to take will be published above the fold on the front page of your newspaper. Would you be proud or ashamed to have your colleagues, family, and friends read about it in stark black and white?

Close your eyes and listen to your intuition.

Imagine telling your partner, your parents, or your child about your decision and actions.

Take a deep breath and get in touch with the sensations of your body and its surroundings.

What is the "right" thing for you to do in this situation?

(If your answer is that you would not be proud to have that article published, perhaps you should reexamine your behavior and look for ways that you can modify it.)

VALUES, PRINCIPLES, AND ETHICAL BOUNDARIES BENEFIT FROM PRACTICE

In this chapter, you identified and operationalized your core values. You did this by uncovering those values that are authentically yours, revealed through the lens of your crucible stories. In order to follow your True North, you need clear indicators that tell you when you are on track and alert when you are not. Through the process of defining actionable leadership principles (values in practice), you began to see what it takes to live your values every day. Finally, clearly defining ethical boundaries helps you avoid those dangerous shades of gray that can sometimes obscure your vision. From here, we move on to explore what truly motivates us and how these are tied to our core values.

KEY TAKEAWAYS

- Your core values are unique to you.
- You may not know what your core values are until they are tested under pressure.

- Dealing with situations where your values conflict reveals which values are most important to you.
- Leadership principles define the way in which you apply your values every day.
- Establishing your ethical boundaries in advance will give you clarity about what to do when you are pushed to the limit.

List of Values

This is not an exhaustive list, and creative versions are welcome.

- Accomplishment, success
- Accountability
- Accuracy
- Adventure
- All for one & one for all
- Beauty
- Calm, quietude, peace
- Challenge
- Change
- Cleanliness, orderliness
- Collaboration
- Commitment
- Communication
- Community
- Competence
- Compassion
- Concern for others
- Courage
- Continuous improvement
- Cooperation
- Coordination
- Country, love of
- Clarity
- Creativity
- Curiosity
- Connectedness
- Decisiveness
- Delight of being, joy
- Democracy
- Discipline
- Discovery
- Ease of Use
- Efficiency
- Equality
- Excellence
- Fairness
- Faith
- Family
- Flair
- Freedom
- Friendship
- Fun
- Global view
- Goodwill
- Goodness
- Gratitude
- Hard work
- Harmony

- Honesty
- Honor
- Independence
- Inner peace, calm, quietude
- Innovation
- Integrity
- Justice
- Knowledge
- Leadership
- Love, romance
- Loyalty
- Maximum utilization (of time, resources)
- Meaning
- Merit
- Money
- Openness
- Peace, nonviolence
- Perfection (of details)
- Personal growth
- Pleasure
- Positive attitude
- Power
- Practicality
- Preservation
- Privacy
- Problem solving
- Progress
- Prosperity, wealth
- Punctuality
- Quality of work
- Regularity

- Resourcefulness
- Respect for others
- Responsiveness
- Results-oriented
- Rule of law
- Safety
- Satisfying others
- Security
- Self-giving
- Self-reliance
- Service (to others, society)
- Simplicity
- Skill
- Speed
- Spirit in life (using)
- Stability
- Standardization
- Status
- Strength to succeed; a will to succeed; achievement
- Systemization
- Teamwork
- Timeliness
- Tolerance
- Tradition
- Tranquillity
- Trust
- Truth
- Unity
- Variety
- Wisdom

SUGGESTED READING

Christensen, C., Allworth, J., and Dillon, K. *How Will You Measure Your Life?* New York: HarperBusiness, 2012.

Gentile, M. *Giving Voice to Values? How to Speak Your Mind When You Know What's Right.* New Haven, CT: New Haven Yale University Press, 2010.

Heifetz, R. *Leadership without Easy Answers.* Cambridge, MA: Belknap, 1994.

Hurley, R. *The Decision to Trust: How Leaders Create High-Trust Organizations.* San Francisco: Jossey-Bass, 2011.

Piper, T., Gentile, M., and Daloz-Parks, S. *Can Ethics Be Taught?* Boston: Harvard Business School Press, 1993.

6

Find Your Sweet Spot

The task of leadership is to create an alignment of strengths,
making our weaknesses irrelevant.
—*Peter Drucker*

There are times when you are good at what you are doing and you are fired up about doing it. You feel as if you are completely in flow. When you find yourself in this position, you have discovered your sweet spot—that point where you are the most alive, most satisfied, and most closely aligned with your True North.

Although we all know what these times are like, they can be hard to find. In Chapter 6 of *Discover Your True North*, Charles Schwab relates that he tried several paths to develop his skills and make his way in the world. For example, tried and abandoned the law before turning to investment research. Despite his many trials, his resilience and persistence did not pay off until he found work that both capitalized on his strength in math and satisfied his drives for independence, financial success, and equal opportunity.

This is one of the promises of *Discovering Your True North Fieldbook:* When you are clear about your strengths and what you love, and when you express them consistently in your leadership, you will be a more effective leader. Why? Because you will spend less time doing things that wear you down and more time doing things that bring you joy. And you will do them to satisfy your inherent drives: your core motivations.

Certainly, there are times when one has to settle for only following a passion or narrowly employing a great skill. But ultimately you should seek to put yourself in a place where you can enjoy both your passions *and* your strengths most of the time.

The key to sustained effectiveness as a leader is to find positions that use your strengths and that are highly motivating to you. We label such positions as "sweet spots." The work in this chapter begins with your motivation to lead.

DISCOVER YOUR INTRINSIC AND EXTRINSIC MOTIVATIONS

Sometimes your motivations are clear and predictable. At other times, you are motivated by deeper forces. To understand your motivations at a deeper level, we will examine two different categories of motivations: intrinsic and extrinsic.

Intrinsic motivations: motivations that have their origins within you and are aligned with your True North.

Extrinsic motivations: motivations that have their origins in the external world.

The terms *intrinsic* and *extrinsic* literally mean "from within" and "from without." Extrinsic motivators include such things as monetary compensation, power, recognition, status, prestigious associations, and other external definitions of success that motivate us. They align closely with our cultural norms of what it means to be successful. Extrinsic motivations are not problematic in themselves. Making money, holding power, and enjoying status and influence can be good things and bring joy, safety, and ease to your life. What is wrong, then, about relying entirely on extrinsic motivations?

All of us are trained well, particularly in the business world, to respond to extrinsic motivations. Yet we may find that in spite of having our material needs fulfilled, we have a nagging feeling that our work lacks a deeper sense of satisfaction. If you are experiencing some of these nagging feelings, you may need to reflect on some of the intrinsic motivations of your leadership.

Leaders often gain insight into their intrinsic motivations during stressful and challenging times, on vacation, or during transitions between assignments. These are all times when we become more introspective.

The purpose of the next two exercises is to help you identify both your extrinsic and intrinsic motivations.

EXERCISE 6.1: YOUR EXTRINSIC MOTIVATIONS

Extrinsic motivations: motivators that have their origins in the external world.

What are your extrinsic motivations? Please fill in Table 6.1 with your unique definition of the extrinsic motivators you identify in your life story. For example, in the monetary compensation category, we have seen a wide range of definitions to include

- Compensation in the top 20 percent of my peers.
- Never have to worry about paying the Visa bill.

Listed below are common extrinsic motivators, the ones that speak most strongly to you (subset of the list) are the ones you will work on. Also, you may have others that are important.

After you have completed your list, rank your extrinsic motivations in order (1 being the most powerful) of their power and importance to you.

Table 6.1: Your Extrinsic Motivations

Category	My Extrinsic Motivations	Rank
1. Monetary compensation		
2. Power		
3. Prestigious title		
4. Public recognition		
5. Social status		
6. Competition		
7. Association with prestigious institutions		
8. Other:		
9. Other:		

Importance of Intrinsic Motivations

Successive stages of leadership carry with them two contrasting challenges. On the one hand, highly capable and experienced leaders are bombarded with increasingly attractive extrinsic motivators. On the other hand, to be an authentic leader you must also be true to your intrinsic motivators.

We are all at risk of being trapped by our success. You may come to think that you are unable to live without a given income or fear that you face insignificance if you step off the fast track to stay in a role that is deeply satisfying. You may fear that you have too much to risk if you pursue your real dreams. These fears can be traps when we give up our authenticity for someone else's idea of what is important.

Many who measure themselves by their public prominence are bedeviled by fears of insignificance, always measuring themselves against those they perceive as competitors. They may be afraid to follow their True North, failing to recognize the risks inherent in not pursuing it. The one-sided pursuit of extrinsic motivations is a trap to the extent that leaders replace intrinsic motivators with extrinsic ones. When leaders trade wealth for satisfaction, recognition for excellence, status for meaning, and winning for their ability to make a difference in the world, they have lost their True North.

Research published in the National Academy of Sciences looked into the power of extrinsic versus intrinsic motivations in predicting or driving career success. They analyzed 11,320 cadets from West Point in terms of their motivations over nine years. They followed them over their careers, and the findings are compelling. Those whose paths employed predominately intrinsic motivations were significantly more likely to graduate, get early promotions, and stay in the Army past their initial five-year term.

So what are your deeply held intrinsic motivations?

Once again, remember that your unique and authentic definitions that speak to you are what we are looking for.

EXERCISE 6.2: YOUR INTRINSIC MOTIVATIONS

Intrinsic motivations: motivators that have their origins within you and are aligned with your True North.

What are your intrinsic motivations? Please fill in Table 6.2 with your unique definitions of intrinsic motivators (subset of the list). For example, in the personal growth and development category, you might say:

- I love learning about human possibilities and learning from those who are willing to share their wisdom. Or,
- I want to deepen my faith and find new ways to express it over my lifespan.

As in Exercise 6.1. notice that your definitions are unique to you; the key is that you define them in a way that is important to you.

Table 6.2: Your Intrinsic Motivations

Category	My Intrinsic Motivations	Rank
1. Engaging in personal growth and development		
2. Doing a good job		
3. Helping others		
4. Leading and organizing others		
5. Being with people you care about		
6. Finding meaning from your efforts		
7. Being true to your beliefs		
8. Making a difference in the world		
10. Influencing others		
11. Other:		
12. Other:		

Listed below are common intrinsic motivators, the ones that speak most powerfully to you (subset of the list) are the ones you will work on. Also, you may have others that are important.

After you have completed your list, rank your intrinsic motivations in order (1 being the most powerful) of relative importance to you.

EXERCISE 6.3: AVOIDING MOTIVATION TRAPS

Both extrinsic and intrinsic motivations are powerful resources. It is natural for human beings to seek recognition and reward, just as it is natural for human beings to search for meaning and connection with others. Both kinds of motivations are important to your authentic leadership when they are linked to your strengths.

If, on the one hand, you try to replace crucial intrinsic motivators with extrinsic ones, you can become unmotivated, dissatisfied, and even bitter. On the other hand, if you deny your need for certain extrinsic motivations, always serving the greater good rather than your own interests, you can become resentful of others' successes, vulnerable to being exploited, and anxious about your financial security.

The purpose of this exercise is to identify potential traps—places where you might stray off course because of an unbalanced pursuit of your motivations. To begin, consider each of the motivations you identified in Tables 6.1 and 6.2. Examine the conditions in your life today under which the service of each of these potential sources of motivation could become a trap. Start with your extrinsic motivations.

When in your life have you been driven primarily by extrinsic motivators? What was the result?

_____

_____

_____

What traps related to focusing too much on your extrinsic motivations can you foresee yourself falling into?

_____

_____

_____

When in your life have you been driven primarily by your intrinsic motivations? What was the result?

_____

_____

_____

Are there any traps related to focusing too much on your intrinsic motivations?

_____

_____

_____

LEADERSHIP STRENGTHS

Next you will consider your greatest leadership strengths and examine how you are putting them to work. Research conducted by the Gallup Leadership Institute, using its StrengthsFinder, has demonstrated that individuals and leaders are most effective and most fulfilled when they are in roles at work that tap into their greatest strengths. These findings are reinforced by the work of positive psychologists Martin Seligman and Mihaly Csikszentmihalyi. This stream of thinking has launched an approach to leadership that places a greater emphasis on putting leaders in positions where they can maximize their unique strengths. This approach is in sharp contrast to past thinking that focused on putting individuals in positions where they were forced to overcome weaknesses.

To complete the next exercises, we will review your life stories to identify those moments when you demonstrated your unique leadership strengths.

EXERCISE 6.4: YOUR MOST POWERFUL LEADERSHIP MOMENTS

In Table 6.3, list the most powerful leadership experiences you have had in your life, including those outside of work as well as when you were young. We want you to pick the moments when you felt proud about who you were as a leader. It's important to consider not only moments of great external success (winning the game, beating the sales forecast by 30 percent, etc.), but to dig deeper and find those moments when it was the internal courage you demonstrated that mattered most (saying the unsaid in a meeting, taking off from work to care for a relative, standing up for your younger sibling, etc.).

Rate each of these experiences (on a scale from 1 to 5, with 5 being the highest) for the degree to which they utilized your intrinsic and extrinsic motivations.

Finally, put a 1 next to the experience that was most satisfying overall, a 2 next to the one that was the next most satisfying, and so on for all the experiences.

After completing this table, examine the patterns of your intrinsic and extrinsic motivations.

Table 6.3: Your Leadership Moments

Leadership Moments	How Much Did It Leverage My Intrinsic Motivations?	How Much Did It Leverage My Extrinsic Motivations?	Most Satisfying

What themes do you see about the importance of your intrinsic and extrinsic motivations across your many leadership moments?

_____

_____

_____

_____

_____

EXERCISE 6.5: DISCOVERING YOUR LEADERSHIP STRENGTHS

In this exercise, you will discover your leadership strengths.

We are looking for a unique set of strengths that show up when you are leading. For example, coauthor Nick Craig's list of key leadership strengths include the following:

- Turns lemons into lemonade with difficult groups of participants
- Integrates the latest concepts into practical applications
- Quickly identifies what is "really" going on in complex situations
- Makes things happen instead of talking about them

In contrast, a senior manager included the following as strengths:

- Running complex processes with large groups
- Coaching several direct reports on multiple projects with ease
- Discovering counterintuitive insights from seemingly disjointed piles of data
- Seeing possibilities where others see none

Look at your list of leadership moments from Table 6.3. Begin to identify and list the unique leadership strengths that are demonstrated in those stories from your past. Then rank your five strongest leadership strengths from 1 to 5, with 1 being your greatest strength.

Table 6.4: My Leadership Strengths

Leadership Strengths	Rank

Reviewing your leadership moments, select one experience that best leveraged your leadership strengths and answer the following question:

Why were you so effective in this situation? How did you feel about yourself at the time?

_____

_____

_____

_____

USING YOUR SWEET SPOT

Aligning your greatest strengths with your most powerful motivations is like flying with a tailwind, paddling with a current, cycling downhill, or driving with high-octane fuel. It is the same state that others call being "in the flow." We call the place where your strengths and motivations come together your "sweet spot," named after the place on a baseball bat, tennis racquet, or golf driver where the most power is transmitted from your swing to the ball. When you hit the sweet spot you know it, even before you start to track the path of the ball.

Your experience is a powerful diagnostic tool for learning where you will excel in the future.

EXERCISE 6.6: DEFINING YOUR SWEET SPOT

Considering the work you have done:

A. List your top 3 extrinsic motivators at this time in your life.

B. List your top 3 intrinsic motivators at this time in your life.

C. List your top 5 leadership strengths.

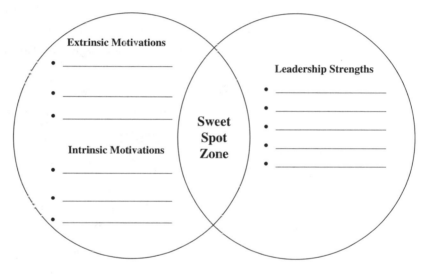

Create a phrase that captures who you are when you are operating from your sweet spot.

_____

_____

_____

_____

YOUR SWEET SPOT TODAY

When you find a role that combines your motivations with your strengths, you have found the sweet spot that will likely maximize your effectiveness in any situation.

EXERCISE 6.7: EXAMINING HOW WELL YOU ARE OPERATING FROM YOUR SWEET SPOT

In this exercise we ask you to consider your present context. In Table 6.4, review the last 12 months and identify each major activity that has taken up at least 5 percent of your workday (meetings you run, meetings you attend, strategic planning, administrative work, classroom participation, case preparation, etc.).

Rank each of the experiences (on a scale from 1 to 5, with 5 being the highest) for the degree to which they utilize your strengths, and then separately rank them for the degree to which you find these experiences motivating. Finally, identify the percentage of time you spend in each these different activities.

Below is an example of a senior HR leader's answer to the exercise (Table 6.5).

Your goal is to spend at least 60 percent of your time in your sweet spot (4–5 score for Strengths/4–5 on Motivations, Table 6.6). That still leaves 30–40 percent of your time to take out the trash," do the laundry, or whatever activities you must do that require attention.

Table 6.5: HR Leader Example

Current Activities	How much does it call on your strengths?	How much does it leverage your motivations?	What percent of your time do you spend on this activity?
Employee Group Presentations	4	5	20 percent
Risk/Compliance Reporting	2	1	10 percent
Strategic Planning	3	3	20 percent
Coaching/Mentoring	4	4	30 percent
Budgeting, Cost Planning	3	2	10 percent

Table 6.6: How Well Are You Operating From Your Sweet Spot

Current Activities	How much does it call on your strengths?	How much does it leverage your motivations?	What percent of your time do you spend on this activity?

Guidelines for Looking at Your Sweet Spot

Actions to Take	When Strengths are . . .	When Motivations are . . .
Increase the amount of time you spend on this. You are highly motivated and you have more to learn/master. Many leaders find this to be the place where they are the happiest.	3–4	5
Welcome to being fully in your sweet spot.	4–5	4–5
For most of us, what once was highly motivating at some point is no longer exciting. After doing it for the 100th time, it no longer satisfies our deeper intrinsic motivations.	4–5	1–3
(Activities in this area are ripe for delegating to others who will find them exciting, or shifting to more of a mentoring/coaching role. We may not be motivated to do the task ourselves, but usually we have a great deal of motivation to develop others!)		

What changes can you make today to spend 10 percent more time in your sweet spot?

_____

_____

_____

EXERCISE 6.8: MAXIMIZING YOUR SWEET SPOT

Imagine/visualize several future situations that would enable you to utilize your sweet spot more fully, then rank them in order from 1 to 5, with 1 being the most satisfying.

Future Situation Envisioned   *Rank*

_____

_____

_____

_____

_____

YOUR SWEET SPOT HOLDS THE KEY TO YOUR EFFECTIVENESS

In this chapter, you have explored how both your intrinsic and extrinsic motivations must be honored.

Next, you linked your motivations with your strengths. In doing so, you identified your sweet spot for leadership. The likelihood of success and fulfillment is far greater when you are operating in a sweet spot. You might identify several sweet spots; the more, the better!

Before we can lead anyone else, we must first learn how to lead ourselves. For many of us, this chapter reveals that we do not spend enough time operating from our sweet spots.

Enlisting the support of those around you can help you excel as an authentic leader. The next chapter, "Build Your Support Team," is devoted to this element of the True North compass.

KEY TAKEAWAYS

- Each leader has a unique set of motivations to lead.
- It is crucial to differentiate between your extrinsic and intrinsic motivations and to understand the potential advantages and disadvantages of each.

- You are at your best—working at or near a sweet spot—when you are highly motivated and tapping into your unique strengths.

- By identifying and unpacking past experiences that were both highly motivating also utilized your greatest strengths, you can learn to identify situations that will enable you to be most effective.

SUGGESTED READING

Ben-Shahar, T. *Being Happy: You Don't Have to Be Perfect to Lead a Richer, Happier Life.* New York: McGraw-Hill, 2010.

Csikszentmihalyi, M. *Flow.* New York: Harper Perennial Modern Classics, 2008.

Pink, D. *Drive.* New York: Riverhead books, 2011.

Seligman, M. *Flourish: A Visionary New Understanding of Happiness and Well-being.* New York: Atria Books, 2011.

7

Build Your Support Team

Don't walk behind me; I may not lead. Don't walk in front of me;
I may not follow. Just walk beside me and be my friend.
—Albert Camus

In this chapter, you will examine how you can build a robust support team to help you along your journey, especially when you are facing great difficulties and challenges.

Leading can be very lonely, especially when things are not going well, and you have no one with whom you can discuss the problems you are facing. Whom do you talk to when you're feeling vulnerable and insecure? Or when you feel that you are at risk of being exposed as an imposter? Or when your ethics and values are being challenged?

Perhaps you fear that others will not maintain confidentiality, or will get so personally involved that you are giving up some of your freedom. Or maybe you feel that they do not understand you or even support you.

Leading can also distort reality for leaders. With leadership comes rewards, recognition, feedback, and appraisals. What you may not recognize is that these things are often presented to leaders with a built-in bias. Subordinates wish to curry favor with their leaders. Yes-men and flatterers are constantly willing to distort or censor what they tell leaders because they want something for themselves.

Even more pervasive is a bias that emerges even when among honest and perceptive people. Leaders are biased toward action, toward existing theories, and toward situations and people that are familiar. However, a leader's bias for action and decisiveness can often have the effect of shutting down or suppressing new ideas or alternative approaches, as people fear challenging powerful leaders.

Finally, leadership is hard. It requires vast stores of energy and commitment. It will use up all the energy you have and still ask for more. Without a support team, leaders are at risk of burning out. At the same time, they must give as much to their relationships as they get from them so that mutually beneficial bonds can develop.

In times like these, having a robust support team around you can be invaluable. When you are most in need of finding direction, your support team helps you get back on track. It sits at the base of your compass, because members of your support team help you stay focused on your True North. Your support team keeps you grounded in reality and provides the support, counsel, and confidence you need as you venture forth to take on the most challenging tasks of your leadership journey.

In the exercises that follow, you will identify members of your personal support group. Right now this group may be a virtual assembly of your intimate friends and family members, or you may have already started to both broaden and deepen your support system. No matter where you are on this important task, you can always improve the amount and quality of those who surround you. Bottom line? While leading can often feel like a lonely task, you definitely do *not* have to go it alone!

EXERCISE 7.1: HOW DO YOU BUILD YOUR SUPPORT TEAM?

The purpose of this exercise is to learn about how you have already drawn support from those around you.

Looking at your life story, think of a time when you most needed support from others.

Who were the key people that supported you the most?

1. _____
2. _____
3. _____
4. _____
5. _____

Identify the five most important supportive people in your life, past and present:

1. _____
2. _____
3. _____
4. _____
5. _____

What was the impact each person had on your life? What might have happened if these people had not been there to support you?

1. _____
2. _____
3. _____
4. _____
5. _____

YOUR MOST IMPORTANT RELATIONSHIP

Your support team should be anchored by at least one person with whom you can be completely vulnerable and open, to whom you can expose all your flaws and still be accepted unconditionally. It could be your spouse, significant other, parent, coach, mentor, best friend, or therapist. Often this person is the only one who can tell you the honest truth when it really matters.

EXERCISE 7.2: YOUR MOST IMPORTANT SUPPORT PERSON

The person you look to most in supporting your leadership is:

_____

_____

This person is important to you because:

_____

_____

_____

You look to this person for support in the following ways:

_____

_____

_____

BUILDING YOUR SUPPORT TEAM

You begin looking for the anchor of your support team in your family because most leaders have their closest relationships with their spouses and family members. These relationships are vitally important because they often provide the unconditional acceptance that leaders find missing in the workplace. Family members can also serve as mirrors that enable you to see yourself as others see you, even if it is fairly humbling. Beyond enabling you to show up ready to lead, your family can be a source of inspiration, a safe group in which to try out your leadership skills, and a source of straight-talking feedback.

EXERCISE 7.3: YOUR FAMILY AS A SUPPORT GROUP

In this exercise, examine the impact of your family of origin—your parents, grandparents, siblings, aunts, uncles, and cousins—as well as your family of choice. The latter includes your spouse or significant other; your children and, possibly your grandchildren; and your in-laws.

What role has your family of origin played in your development as a leader? In what ways have they supported you through difficult challenges and helped you grow?

_____

_____

_____

What role does your family of choice play in your life, and specifically in your development as a leader? What have they done to support you during challenges? What kinds of feedback have they offered to help you improve your leadership skills?

_____

_____

_____

DEVELOPING A MENTOR

Have you had a particular teacher, coach, supervisor, or adviser who has been influential in your interest in leadership and your development as a leader? This is your leadership mentor.

Leadership mentors are the figures in your life who help you develop leadership skills and build your judgment and confidence as a leader. The best mentors do not necessarily have all the answers for you. Instead, they have the ability to ask probing questions that broaden your perspective on the issues you are facing and serve as a reality test for you, especially when you are in denial, distorting reality, or projecting your personal problems onto someone else. As leadership guru Warren Bennis says, "Denial and projection are the enemies of reality."

What many aspiring leaders fail to realize is that mentoring relationships need to go both ways to be lasting and mutually beneficial. In this way, they can provide both the mentor and the person being mentored with opportunities to learn and grow while working toward common goals.

Don't stop at one mentor, and don't think that your mentor or mentors must have the ultimate answers to important issues in your life. You are unique; your best learning will come from multiple sources. The more diverse your sources of learning, the better. In the end, however, you have to make the final decisions about your mentors and the degree to which you are willing to include them in your leadership journey.

EXERCISE 7.4: YOUR MENTORING RELATIONSHIPS

The purpose of this exercise is to discover how you have benefited from mentors in your leadership development.

The following people have helped mentor you over the years:

1. _____
2. _____
3. _____
4. _____
5. _____

Which mentor has been most important to you in your development as a leader? In what ways has this person interacted with you and helped you develop?

_____

_____

_____

_____

DEVELOPING GENUINE FRIENDSHIPS

One of the first areas of life to be cut back by busy leaders is their friendships. When things are going well and time is short, it is tempting to overlook long-term friends who have been with you through good times and bad. Friendships, after all, require maintenance, time spent together, and the cultivation of mutual interests. When your work is demanding more and more of you and putting a strain on your family, where can you find the time for friends? These are the times when you most need your friends, because they will be among the most useful reality checks and sources of support in your life.

When leaders are doing well, they are surrounded by people clamoring to be their friends. Everyone is calling to have lunch or dinner or to come to a party or a ball game with them. At those times, many leaders find it extremely difficult to determine whether a prospective friend is the real deal. But when leaders go through a down period, when they suffer career or personal setbacks, those fair-weather friends are likely to disappear, leaving only the tried and true as sources of support, reality testing, and contact with the world.

EXERCISE 7.5: USING YOUR FRIENDS TO SUPPORT YOU

How important are your friends in helping you become a better leader? Do you have friends with whom you can openly share the challenges you face?

Who are your three most trusted friends to whom you would turn if you really needed help are?

1. _____

2. _____

3. _____

A friendship that has been mutually beneficial over an extended period of time is:

_____

_____

_____

You made this friendship meaningful and enduring in the following ways:

_____

_____

_____

Describe a time of trial or crisis in your life when you turned to a friend or friends for help.

During this crisis, your friend was helpful to you in the following ways:

_____

_____

_____

Describe a time when you have been helpful to a friend who was in need of advice or help.

You were helpful to your friend in the following ways:

_____

_____

_____

Describe a relationship that did not work for which you feel some degree of responsibility.

Describe why this relationship did not work out for you:

_____

_____

_____

If you had the opportunity to do it over again, you would do things differently in the following ways:

_____

_____

_____

Creating a Personal/True North Support Group

A personal/True North support group can be one of the most valuable and rewarding methods of support on the journey of authentic leadership. Typically, such a group consists of six to eight people who meet on a regular basis to discuss important issues in their lives. The group works best when a regular schedule and meeting place are established and the group has a program or agenda for each meeting.

Ideally, the group rotates leadership for each meeting so that each member has responsibility for developing the program in advance, even sharing readings or exercises with group members to prepare before they meet. This workbook is designed for just that purpose. (For further information on how to form such a group, refer to *True North Groups* by Bill George and Doug Baker.)

Your personal support group can help identify your True North and help redirect you when you are getting off track. In turn, by sharing your insights, you can do the same for them, as all relationships must be mutually beneficial to be sustainable.

EXERCISE 7.6: YOUR PERSONAL/TRUE NORTH SUPPORT GROUP

Have you had a personal support group? If so, describe its value and meaning to you and your leadership. If you have never had such a group, would you like to form one? If so, what kind of people would you like to have in your group?

Your personal/True North support group is:

_____

_____

_____

Its value and meaning to you is:

_____

_____

_____

You would like to form a support group with the following kinds of people:

_____

_____

_____

CREATING A PERSONAL BOARD OF DIRECTORS

Finally, it's time to identify your personal board of directors. Businesses create boards to guide their organizations and leaders. Even privately held companies and family-owned businesses establish boards. Given where you are right now on your leadership journey, do you have the mentors and advisers necessary to advise and direct you?

Usually it's when we need one the most that we realize it isn't really in place. While your personal/True North group can include people from all walks of life, your board of directors is more about helping you step into your authentic leadership within the current work/professional challenges you are facing.

A personal board of directors should be comprised of key mentors and wise leaders who have been on a similar journey to yours, but are further down the path. They truly know what it's like to be in your shoes and to face the decisions, challenges, and opportunities that you're dealing with now.

EXERCISE 7.7: BUILDING A PERSONAL BOARD OF DIRECTORS

The purpose of this exercise is to identify your personal board of directors. You must determine the combination of mentors and advisers that would be most helpful to you at this point in your life. Consider including both people that you see on a regular basis and those you meet with two to three times a year. These people should have either a deep understanding of your professional world or have known you for a long time. A key criterion is that they should be more focused on who you are becoming as a leader versus who you were in the past.

Your personal board of directors for this phase of your journey includes:

Name	Frequency of dialogue	Date next meeting
1.		
2.		
3.		
4.		
5.		
6.		

THE BENEFITS OF YOUR SUPPORT TEAM

In this chapter, you have had a chance to assess and develop your support team. Our advice is to think through the kinds of people you need in your support system and then build it gradually. With each individual, it is important to develop trust and confidentiality. Doing so takes time, but it will pay off when you need it most.

Remember, there will be many times when members of your support team will be the only ones who will tell you when you have lost sight of your True North.

In the next chapter, Integrate Your Life, you will address the central challenge of how to be the same person in all areas of your life.

KEY TAKEAWAYS

- Your support team is a necessary element for sustaining you on your journey as an authentic leader.
- Build your support team early and include those people who know you well and can be honest with you.
- You have people in your life today who have been and should remain core members of your support team.
- People whom you have met after you have become a more powerful leader may have biases that make them inappropriate for your support team.
- Each phase of your leadership development should have a new leadership mentor.
- Assembling a personal board of directors is a significant step on your journey.
- Having a longstanding support group will help you keep sight of your True North.

SUGGESTED READING

George, Bill, *True North Groups*. San Francisco, CA: Berrett-Koehler Publishers, 2011.
Gladwell, M. *The Tipping Point: How Little Things Can Make a Big Difference*. New York: Little, Brown, 2000.
Krzyzewski, M. *Leading with the Heart*. New York: Warner Books, 2000.
Peck, M. S. *The Road Less Traveled*. New York: Simon & Schuster, 1979.

8

Integrate Your Life

One Saturday afternoon in 2007, I was working on the
previous edition of this chapter on integrating your life.
Keely, my 9-year-old, came up to me and asked what I was doing.
When I told her, she paused, then grabbed me and said, "I am bored,
and you're coming with me as you need to live it versus just writing about it."

—*Nick Craig (coauthor)*

To lead an integrated life is to bring together all major elements of your personal life and your professional life so that you can be the same person everywhere, all the time—perhaps as good a definition of being authentic as there is.

After working with thousands of very successful leaders from around the world, we have witnessed how challenging it is to create an integrated life. Being world class at work at some point ends up being the easy part. We know where our sweet spot is at work; however, replicating it in the other parts of our life becomes increasingly important as we hit the inevitable speed bumps we call "life."

We want to draw an important distinction here. Integration is not a code word for work/life *balance*. Balance implies adjustments to keep everything in one's life in a perfect equilibrium: "Okay, a little bit on this side and a little bit on that side . . . whoops, a little less over there . . . okay, now switch this for that." We've watched countless leaders try this balancing act and wind up deeply dissatisfied.

The drawbacks to the idea of balancing are subtle but pervasive. Your attention is constantly drawn to the act of balancing rather than to life as a whole. With half-measures and adjustments, none of the aspects of your life are truly served. Perhaps most important, you are constantly moving between separate domains, carrying all the baggage of the different personae, responsibilities, and effort that such juggling entails.

Instead, let's be authentic about how our lives unfold over time. Most of us follow a similar trajectory: We go to college, begin our careers, get married, have children, change jobs, experience advances and setbacks, and prepare for retirement. During each of these phases, one aspect of our lives (professional, family, personal, community/friends) requires more focus than the others. The opportunity lies in discovering where our focus should be. When work isn't great, our kids and friends become an oasis; when things are challenging at home, work picks up the slack.

The grounding that comes with an integrated life can help you avoid being too cocky during high points in your work and too stressed and agitated during low points. We believe the vision and perspective that comes from living an integrated life is essential to sustaining high performance and to turning setbacks into opportunities.

Integrating your life is quite often about making courageous choices.

This is a message that may be difficult to hear, particularly for those who enjoy an endless array of opportunities and easy choices. You have been successful, and you want to have it all—right now! If you do not feel some discomfort when you think about this, you may not be getting the point.

Integration involves saying yes and no to yourself on the basis of your True North. This is harder than you might think. When a plum opportunity comes your way with increases in income, power, status, and recognition, will you be prepared to say no? Put differently, will you be prepared to say yes to something important in your life and speak up for it?

Some of the most powerful crucible stories we have heard from leaders contain a recurring theme: making a wrong decision outside of their professional life. In each case, what they learned about their own fall from grace and what it took to reestablish an authentically integrated life had a huge impact on how they led from that point forward.

Our goal in this chapter is to help you see your unique path of living an integrated life so you don't need a crucible to remind you of your True North!

THE BUCKETS OF YOUR LIFE

Let's begin by taking stock of each of the major areas of your life: work life, personal life, family life, and friends and community.

We're going to use the metaphor of buckets of water to represent each of these important areas of your life. Assume you have a limited quantity of water—your time, your energy, your spirit. You have several buckets to fill, but you don't have enough water to fill them all. Do you fill each of them partway and monitor them closely for leaks? Or do you put all your water in one or two buckets, to the exclusion of the others?

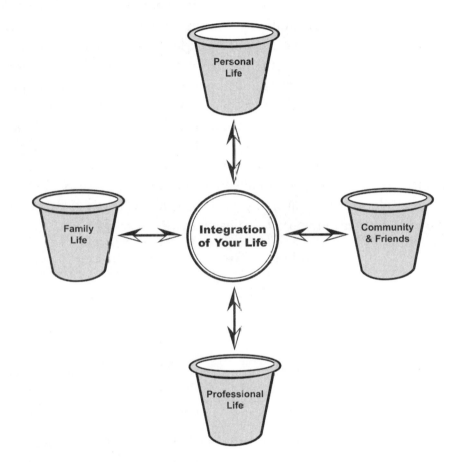

EXERCISE 8.1: THE BUCKETS OF YOUR LIFE

Let's examine how you can bring together all aspects of your life into an integrated whole in order to live your life with integrity. The underlying belief here is that in doing so, you will be a more effective leader and lead a more satisfying and fulfilling life.

First, examine the most challenging life/leadership experiences and your life today to determine which areas, represented by the buckets, need attention.

As a starting point, we recommend evaluating all four buckets in no set order of priority: your personal life, your community and friends, your professional life, and your family life. Although filling the buckets in your life to the desired levels may seem deceptively simple at first glance, it is a lot more difficult than it seems.

Also, if you're wondering what we mean by personal life, you are not alone. For many of us, the challenge of working and raising a family exhausts most of our resources. Spending time on something that we really love doing (singing, playing the piano, reading, running, etc.) and is just for us seems like an undeserved luxury. These types of activities are often the last to get our attention, yet they are also the ones that replenish us. Some of our most successful alumni rank these activities as the most critical to their ability to be effective in challenging times. We will help you assess where your personal life activities should fit.

Let's look at the status of your buckets today. In Table 8.1, begin by describing the amount of attention you give to each area of your life.

Table 8.1: The Buckets of Your Life

Bucket	Attention Given (percent)	Attention Desired (percent)
Professional life		
Personal life		
Family life		
Community and friends		

Note: The percentages for all columns should add up to 100.

In the left-hand column, write the percentage of time you devote to the four areas now. In the right-hand column, write the percentage of time you would like to devote to each area.

Which buckets do you need to direct attention to now, to honor your True North?

_____

_____

_____

Which of these buckets are you prepared to cut back on in order to make room in your life for one of the buckets that is too empty?

_____

_____

_____

What actions will most contribute to you doing just that?

_____

_____

_____

EXERCISE 8.2: ASPECTS OF YOUR INTEGRATED LIFE

The purpose of this exercise is to design an integrated approach to your life based on the actual state of your buckets and the ways in which they sustain you and your leadership.

Let's start with your personal life.

The most important aspects of your personal life are:

_____

_____

_____

How do you set time aside for yourself and for your personal development? In what ways do you nurture your inner life?

_____

_____

_____

Consider how mindfulness as well as religious and spiritual practices fit into your buckets. You are not the first person to grapple with questions of purpose and values, working to discern the best reasons for making choices and struggling to be a whole person. These are age-old questions that are at the core of most spiritual and religious practices. Today's mindfulness disciplines (meditation, stopping and being present in the moment, daily gratitude exercises, mindfulness, running, etc.) are nonsecular expressions that we continue to find value in.

It is important to develop those introspective practices that enable you to relax and reflect on your life. Research shows that humans are designed to have a negative bias toward events. Expecting the negative has been critical to our survival in earlier times. The need to step back and reframe our experiences, to see the positive and compelling story that is ours to capture, is a discipline all authentic leaders need. In some ways the most important question we must answer in challenging times is, "What does this mean?" You can answer it from the surface of the moment and it will sound like the weather report. Or as a result of having reflected on similar moments, you can provide a deeper insight that will help others do the same, and it will sound like the actual weather!

Do you have regular religious or spiritual practices? In what ways do they contribute to accessing your deeper wisdom when it's most needed?

_____

_____

_____

What mindfulness practice have you found that helps you to step back and see the bigger picture?

_____

_____

_____

When faced with difficult news in any part of your life, what have you done that helps you stay grounded?

_____

_____

_____

Next, turn to your family life.

Your family grounds you, no matter who you are and no matter what your relationships are with them. Family members have a secret back door into your authentic self. Although you may at times want to lock and bolt that door forever—as when your child's timetable for your attention does not fit your scheduled meeting—family members may help you get back to your True North when you most need it.

When you are at the top of your game and feeling like the master of the universe, your family reminds you that can never remember where you put the car keys or your wallet. And when you are really down on yourself, they know your whole story, seeing beyond the present moment, and are there to support you.

What are the most important aspects of your family life?

_____

_____

_____

In what ways will your life and time commitments change as you take on additional family commitments?

1. _____

2. _____

3. _____

How do you manage your family's time requirements and conflicts between your family's needs and the requirements of your work?

_____

_____

_____

Turn next to your friendships and your community.

Your friends and community are also potentially important sources of grounding. You are more likely to encounter diversity of life's experiences among this wider circle than within your intimate family or narrow work circle. By getting to know fellow pilgrims on their journeys, regardless of what they do in the world, you will become a more compassionate person and a better leader.

What role do friendships play in your life? Do you look to your friends for regular counsel and advice on challenging issues you are facing? How much time do you devote to developing and nurturing your friendships?

_____

_____

_____

_____

_____

_____

Is your community an integral part of your life? In what ways do you serve your community? How does community service help you become a better leader?

_____

_____

_____

_____

_____

_____

In what ways would you like to serve your community in the future?

1. _____
2. _____
3. _____
4. _____
5. _____

Finally, turn to your professional life.

Living an integrated life means that your professional life is simply one part of a greater whole. Some see the other parts of their lives as a distraction to be tolerated, as they dedicate themselves to their professional lives. In our view, living an integrated life provides the opportunity to take your professional life to a whole new level of collaboration and integration with all that makes you whole.

What will you do to ensure that you stay grounded professionally?

1. _____
2. _____
3. _____
4. _____
5. _____

In what ways do your family life, personal life, friendships, and community life contribute to your professional life?

1. _____
2. _____
3. _____
4. _____
5. _____

How will you cope with the seductions and pressures of professional life and still focus on your True North?

1. _____

2. _____

3. _____

4. _____

5. _____

MEASURING SUCCESS IN YOUR LIFE

As you practice living a grounded life you should ask yourself, "How do I define success in my life?" Often the externally defined measures of success pull our lives out of alignment and prevent us from leading an integrated life. What measures do you use?

EXERCISE 8.3: MEASURING SUCCESS IN YOUR LIFE

The purpose of this exercise is to examine how you measure success.

How do you measure success in your life right now? Where do these metrics come from?

_____

_____

_____

_____

At the end of your days, how will you measure success in your life?

_____

_____

_____

_____

Think about your experiences of happiness. We define happiness as feelings of pleasure or contentment.

What would bring you the greatest amount of happiness in your life?

_____

_____

_____

_____

Think about your desires for achievement, those important goals that you strive for.

What are the long-term achievements you would like to realize in your life?

_____

_____

_____

_____

Now consider your desire for significance in your life. We define significance as the extent to which you've made a positive impact on people you care about.

How would you define significance in your life? What is the positive impact on others that you would like to have?

_____

_____

_____

_____

INTEGRATING YOUR LIFE

Integrating your life entails choices and trade-offs. You should make those choices and trade-offs in a way that is intentional and fits your life.

EXERCISE 8.4: INTEGRATING YOUR LIFE

The purpose of this exercise is to assemble a vision of your integrated life that fits your life and your leadership. Start with your experience of making choices and trade-offs between various aspects of your life.

What is the most difficult choice or trade-off that you have had to make in the past?

_____

_____

_____

_____

What would you do differently based on what you now know about your True North?

_____

_____

_____

_____

What is the most difficult choice or trade-off that you are facing right now?

_____

_____

_____

_____

Living and leading with integrity results from integrating your life, so that you can be one person and be true to that person no matter what setting you are in. Think of your life as a house, with a den for your personal life, a study for your professional life, a family room for your family, and a living room to share with your friends.

Can you knock down the walls between the rooms in your life and be the same person in all aspects?

_____

_____

_____

_____

Are you able to be the same authentic person in each environment, or do you behave differently at work compared to the way you act at home, with your friends, or in your community?

_____

_____

_____

_____

PRIORITIZING WHAT YOU LOVE DOING

Now it's time to go one level below what you may have uncovered so far. Yes, everything you have defined is really important to living an integrated life. In most cases, however, there is one thing missing—one thing that makes the whole journey worth living and without which externally it will look great and at times you will be fooled as well, but other times it will be the missing link.

EXERCISE 8.5: DOING WHAT YOU LOVE

The purpose of this exercise is to remind you of those activities you just love doing that aren't about anyone else or achieving some external goals that others value. It's time to give space to some of the activities you really love doing for yourself.

The options range from singing, drawing, playing the piano, or cooking, to shopping for that special 100th pair of shoes! Whatever the activity, it brings you great joy and personal satisfaction.

What are the two to three things that you love doing for yourself that you can either bring back or begin to do in your life?

_____

_____

_____

_____

When are you going to do it and whom should you tell, so you have someone who will help you be accountable for making it happen?

_____

_____

_____

_____

What changes do you need to make in your life for this activity to be a constant companion on your journey?

_____

_____

_____

_____

REFLECTING ON YOUR JOURNEY

For many of us, this chapter is the hardest, but it may have the most important message of all in enabling us to sustain our authentic leadership. Our invitation is for you to consciously choose the amount of time and energy you devote to each part of your life. Each of us will have a different mix that fits our values, motivations, capabilities, and current situation.

In this chapter, you also explored your own criteria for success, happiness, achievement, and significance. Applying these criteria to your life enables you to choose the appropriate amount of time and energy to invest in each aspect of your life.

In Part Two of this guide, you have worked through the five developmental areas of the True North compass. Now you are ready to move on to Part Three, which will enable you to put your authentic leadership into action.

KEY TAKEAWAYS

- An integrated life evens out the highs and lows of leadership and therefore supports your authenticity as a leader in all circumstances.
- The buckets of your life are unique to your life.
- Each bucket of your life helps ground you in different ways. Each, therefore, helps you be more effective as a leader.
- If your criteria for measuring success in your life are going to fit your True North, they must also be unique to your life.
- Being the same person, with the same values, goals, and motivations in all areas of your life, is a necessary element for following your True North.
- Finding time to do the things you really love is part of living your True North!

SUGGESTED READING

Christensen, C., Allworth, J., and Dillon, K. *How Will You Measure Your Life?* New York: HarperBusiness, 2012.

Harris, D. *10 Percent Happier: How I Tamed the Voice in My Head, Reduced Stress without Losing My Edge, and Found Self-Help That Actually Works—a True Story.* New York: HarperCollins, 2014.

Sandberg, Sheryl. *Lean In: Women, Work, and the Will to Lead.* New York: Knopf, 2013.

Williams, M. and Penman, D. *Mindfulness: An Eight-Week Plan for Finding Peace in a Frantic World.* Emmaus, PA: Rodale Books, 2011.

Part Three

Put Your Authentic Leadership into Action

In Part Two, you worked on all five elements of your leadership compass. Now you will focus on applying these insights in order to lead with purpose, empower others, and become a global leader. As a bridge between your developmental work here and emerging real life as an authentic leader, we conclude with an exercise that summarizes and integrates everything you've learned into an actionable personal development plan.

9

The Transformation from I to We

> Good leaders must first become good servants.
> —*Robert Greenleaf*, The Servant as Leader

THE END OF THE HEROIC LEADER

We've all seen this pattern in our bosses, subordinates, and colleagues: They have all the right skills, use the latest management tools, articulate the right messages with the most popular buzzwords, and espouse the right strategies. But underneath something seems to be missing. Followers respond with caution. Supervisors are worried, but can't quite pin down what's wrong. Even concerned friends keep their distance. All the pieces seem to be there, and yet these leaders are never able to rally sustained support from their teams. This is because they lead from a predominantly "I" orientation.

Leaders often begin their careers with a primary focus on themselves—their performance, achievements, and rewards. As they enter the world of work, they see themselves in the image of an all-conquering hero who can change the world for the better. The early years of leaders' lives are often spent in education and skill development, which leads to contributions being made mostly as individuals.

You might think that the archetypal hero would be a natural model for an organizational leader. We learned from our interviews with authentic leaders that the hero stage is a useful starting point, but many leaders have difficulty in moving beyond it. As young leaders are promoted from roles as individual contributors to managers, many believe they are being recognized for their heroic abilities to produce results.

"We spend our early years trying to be the best," said Jaime Irick of General Electric. "To get into West Point or General Electric, you have to be the best. That is defined by what you can do on your own—your ability to be a phenomenal analyst or consultant or do well on a standardized test."

In spite of all the accolades received for heroic performance, young leaders eventually reach a point in their journeys where this approach no longer works. They become overwhelmed; the sheer volume of work becomes too much for them; others no longer respond to their "heroic efforts" and something needs to change.

As leaders hit this developmental wall, the first seeds of transforming from "I" to "We" are planted. Initial success may reinforce what leaders did at an early stage, but difficult times eventually force them to question this approach. At some point, authentic leaders begin to rethink what their life and leadership are all about. They may start by asking, "Do I have to do it all *myself*?" "Why can't I get this team to achieve the goals I have set forth?" For some, the transformation to becoming an authentic leader results from the positive experience of having a wise mentor or having a unique opportunity at a young age. But as much as all of us want positive experiences like these, for most of us, the difficult transformation from "I" to "We" happens only when the hero in us stumbles or falls.

When experiencing the transformation from "I" to "We," leaders are faced with a powerful paradox. Their current orientation has gotten them where they are today. They've been rewarded over and over again for their individual contributions. It's incredibly hard to let go of an approach that has served them so well for so long.

When I'm (Scott) teaching MBA students, at the start of a semester, I frequently make the following offer: "We have a choice in our approach to graded work in this course. With a show of hands, how many of you want to do a group project?" Crickets . . . not only does no one raise them, many students actually sit on their hands. "What? No takers? Why not?" Eventually, some brave soul shares the obvious: "We don't want to be evaluated based on what others do; at least I don't. I want my grade to be based on my own work, not my classmates'. Besides, do you know how hard it is to get anything done in a group?"

At this point, I remind them why they're here: "The mission of Harvard Business School is to 'educate leaders who make a difference in the world,' and you all just signed on to take a course about leadership, right?" This generates some quizzical looks, and more than a few eyes roll. I continue: "No doubt you all wrote admissions essays attempting to convince HBS that you aspire to be such leaders, ones who make a difference, yes?" Nods. I continue: "You do realize that as leaders you will be evaluated on what *other* people accomplish, and not you, right?" Stunning, frightened silence. It's as if these incredibly accomplished, exceptionally bright students, for the very first time, considered the possibility that leading might not be just about them.

As part of Harvard Business School's Centennial Celebration in 2008, Harvard University President Drew Faust delivered a poignant speech suggesting a slight change to the wording of the HBS mission statement, a change consistent with the shift from "I" to "We." Delivered in the midst of a horrific worldwide financial crisis, her words took on special meaning. Here are selected excerpts from that speech. You can find a link to her entire speech in the references at the end of this chapter.

As HBS today states its mission: "We educate leaders who make a difference in the world." This mission has a new urgency. Until now business school students have graduated with great confidence. They joined the fraternity of "masters of the universe," as Tom Wolfe named them in *Bonfire of the Vanities*. They created a world in which the market became the organizing metaphor. Today, markets are disordered, and we are working frantically to fix a broken financial system. Never have we more needed leaders who make a difference. But how do we shape them and how do we determine the sort of difference they will make?

For 100 years, HBS has strived to situate technical expertise within a broader vision, an intellectually curious approach to the problems of business. Leadership that makes a difference in the world. . . . This is a matter of both values and vision—of a commitment to purposes beyond one's self but also a grasp of wider imperatives and understandings. Leaders are accountable for more than themselves; they must be both willing and able to accept that responsibility.

Every part of Harvard commits itself to generating leaders. But leadership is a means; it is not an end in itself. It must be about more than the distinction or excellence of the leaders. A focus on leadership must not become an exercise in self-satisfaction or congratulation. Leaders exist to serve followers, and leaders' successes must be measured not simply by their power to move others, but by the directions in which they take those who follow them.

Business education . . . has the opportunity to produce not just leaders that make a difference *in* the world, but leaders who make a difference *for* the world. That should be the goal for both HBS and Harvard University in the century to come.

—Drew Gilpin Faust, President, Harvard University

Only when you stop focusing on your own ego will you be able to develop other leaders. You will be able to move beyond being competitive with talented peers and subordinates, and you will be more open to other points of view. As you overcome your need to control everything or do everything yourself, you find that people are more interested in working with you. A lightbulb goes on as you recognize the unlimited potential of empowered leaders working together toward a shared purpose. This transformation opens the door to discovering your full potential as an authentic leader.

As GE's Irick went on to say: "If you want to be a leader, you've got to flip that switch and understand that it's about serving the folks on your team. This is a very simple concept, but one that many people overlook. The sooner people realize it, the faster they will grow into leaders."

The transformation from "I" to "We" is the true point of embarkation on the leader's journey. It propels you into the next stage as the hero's journey is left behind and the true leader's journey begins.

Your Arrow Must Be Pointing Away

Remember those incredibly sophisticated "scratch-and-sniff" meters we have? When it comes to measuring our leaders, the first and most obvious attribute we sniff out is whether their arrows are pointing away or curving back on themselves.

Have you ever seen leaders where it's all about them, their careers, their success? "*We* need to get this done so that *we* hit our numbers and *I* get promoted." Of course, no sane leader ever says this (at least not out loud), but many of us have experienced situations where it's painfully obvious that leaders' primary reason for leading is to further their own careers. They lead from a self-centered "I" orientation; their arrows point directly back at themselves.

Then there are those leaders who enlist our efforts in causes greater than themselves, whose leadership starts with others first. Their "arrows" are pointing away; they are selfless, not self-centered. These are the leaders Robert Greenleaf describes in a series of now-classic essays titled *Servant Leadership*. After reading Hermann Hesse's short novel *The Journey to the East*, Greenleaf concluded that great leaders are first experienced as servants. Their initial instinct and primary motivation is to help others.

The servant-leader is servant first. It begins with the natural feeling that one wants to serve. Then conscious choice brings one to aspire to lead. The best test is: Do those served grow as persons; do they, while being served, become healthier, wiser, freer, more autonomous, more likely themselves to become servants?

Ego focuses on one's own survival, pleasure, and enhancement to the exclusion of others; ego is selfishly ambitious. It sees relationships in terms of threat or no threat, like little children who classify all people as "nice" or "mean." Conscience, on the other hand, both democratizes and elevates ego to a larger sense of the group, the whole, the community, the greater good. It sees life in terms of service and contribution, in terms of others' security and fulfillment.

—Robert K. Greenleaf, *Servant Leadership*

EXERCISE 9.1: HOW IT FEELS TO BE LED FROM DIFFERENT ORIENTATIONS

Our transformation from "I" to "We" often starts by observing others, by reflecting on how we experience leaders whose arrows are pointing away or back at themselves. We learn not only from leaders we admire, but also from those we find to be wanting. In this exercise, we'll ask you to recall what it felt like to be led from different orientations.

Think of a time when you felt micromanaged, when you worked for someone who led primarily from an "I" orientation, someone whose arrow was pointing firmly back at themselves. Describe what it felt like. What impact did your leader's orientation have on your level of engagement and commitment? What impact did it have on your motivation to lead?

_____

_____

_____

_____

_____

_____

_____

_____

_____

_____

_____

_____

Now think of a time when you felt empowered, when you worked for someone who led primarily from a "We" orientation, someone whose arrow was pointing away, someone who enlisted your efforts in something larger than either themselves or yourself. Describe what it felt like. What impact did this leader's orientation have on your level of engagement and commitment? What impact did it have on your motivation to lead?

_____

_____

_____

_____

_____

_____

_____

_____

_____

_____

When reflecting on our experience with other leaders, it's uncomfortably obvious how their orientation impacts us as followers. However, for some reason, what we see so clearly in others is often not as clear when we turn the spotlight on ourselves. The next exercise asks you to do just that: When it comes to this shift from "I" to "We," how do you think others experience your leadership?

EXERCISE 9.2: WHERE AM I IN MOVING FROM "I" TO "WE"?

No doubt there are times when you are "We" oriented. However, if you're like most of us, there are also times when that arrow bends right back onto yourself. It's important to understand how much of your time is spent leading from each orientation, and whether or not you can lead from the orientation you need, when you need it. The purpose of this exercise is to learn where you are in this fundamental shift from "I" to "We."

Looking at your life story, describe a time when you were leading from an "I" orientation.

_____

_____

_____

_____

_____

_____

_____

Describe a time when you were leading from a "We" orientation.

_____

_____

_____

_____

_____

_____

In leading from a "We" orientation, what impact did you have on others and on the results you wanted to achieve? How did this compare with the "I" orientation?

_____

_____

_____

_____

_____

_____

_____

What percentage of your time is currently marked by leading from the "We" orientation? What percentage of your time should this be?

_____

Leading from "We": At present_____ percent.   In the future_____ percent. What steps can you take to lead more consistently from a "We" orientation?

1. _____

2. _____

3. _____

4. _____

5. _____

GUIDING YOUR LEADERSHIP DEVELOPMENT

If your leadership journey is simply to become more authentic, gain greater clarity about who you are, your strengths and motivations, then it is incomplete. At some point you have to ask yourself the deeper questions: To what end? In the service of what? Why am I leading? If indeed it's mostly about you, then you are still firmly anchored in the initial stages of leading. You have yet to make that fundamental and all-important shift from "I" to "We."

People rarely respond to leaders whose arrows point back at themselves. If you want to enlist the efforts of others—really, deeply engage them—it must be in pursuit of a cause that is not only greater than your own, but also greater than theirs. In the next chapter, we'll help you address perhaps the most fundamental question in your journey: What is the purpose of your leadership?

KEY TAKEAWAYS

- The era of heroic leaders is gone.
- The first significant developmental transformation in our leadership journey involves a fundamental shift in orientation: from "I" to "We."
- The shift from "I" to "We" involves a significant reframing of our identity from that of a valued individual contributor to seeing ourselves as a servant-leader who empowers others.
- If our arrows are *not* pointing away, others will know it. This is one of the most obvious and potentially destructive attributes found in young leaders.
- Becoming a more authentic leader is not enough. We must be clear about why we lead. Our journey has to be about more than just ourselves.

SUGGESTED READING

Campbell, J. *The Hero's Journey*. Novato, Calif.: New World Library, 1990.

Faust, D. H. Harvard Business School Centennial speech. http://www.harvard.edu/president/speech/2008/harvard-business-school-centennial, Cambridge, October 14, 2008.

Greenleaf, R. K. *Servant Leadership: A Journey into the Nature of Legitimate Power and Greatness*. Mahwah, NJ: Paulist Press, 1977.

Hesse, H. *The Journey to the East*. New York: Picador, 1956.

Hill, L. *Becoming a Manager: How New Managers Master the Challenges of Leadership*. Boston: Harvard Business School Publishing, 2003.

Mackey, J. and Sisodia, R. *Conscious Capitalism*. Boston: Harvard Business School Publishing, 2014.

Mandela, N. R. *Long Walk to Freedom: The Autobiography of Nelson Mandela*. Boston: Back Bay Books, 1994.

Maslow, A. *Maslow on Management*. Hoboken, NJ: John Wiley & Sons, 1998.

Quinn, R. E. *Building the Bridge as You Walk on It: A Guide for Leading Change*. San Francisco: Jossey-Bass, 2004.

Smith, D. K. *On Value and Values: Thinking Differently About We in an Age of Me.* Upper Saddle River, NJ: Prentice Hall, 2004.

Snook, S. A. and Khurana, R. K. "The End of the Great Man." In *The Essential Bennis*, Warren Bennis, ed. San Francisco: Jossey-Bass, 2009, 138–159.

Spears, L. C. and Lawrence, M. eds *Focus on Leadership: Servant-Leadership for the Twenty-First Century.* Hoboken, NJ: John Wiley and Sons, 2002.

Useem, M. *The Leadership Moment.* New York: Three Rivers Press, 1998.

10

Lead with Purpose

> "The two most important days in your life are the day
> you are born and the day you find out why."
> —*Mark Twain*

After working through the previous chapters in this guide, you are now prepared to understand and lead from your purpose. Your leadership purpose is the unique gift that you bring to the world. No matter what job, title, or occupation you hold, your leadership purpose is the magic that defines who you are as a leader. Although your leadership *style* may vary as you change roles from parent to manager to community volunteer, your leadership *purpose* will remain unchanged. All of the people you lead, regardless of age or title, see the same unique value you bring to their world: your purpose.

Probably the simplest way to understand your leadership purpose is to ask the following question: "If I were to disappear from my current job/role in life and someone else with equivalent skills were to take my place, what would people miss?" The answer to that question would be a clear expression of your leadership purpose.

Since writing the original version of this book, there has been an explosion of interest in purpose. Martin Seligman, the father of positive psychology, has described purpose as a pathway to flourishing in one's life. Daniel Pink argues in his book *Drive* that purpose is one of three keys to exceptional performance in the twenty-first century. Harvard Business School research on what helps female leaders make it to the top concludes that clarity of one's purpose is essential. Doctors have even found that people are 2.5 times less likely to experience the symptoms Alzheimer's disease if they have purpose in their lives.

As Viktor Frankl wrote in *Man's Search for Meaning*—one of the 10 most significant books ever written, according to the Library of Congress—happiness cannot be pursued; it ensues as the result of living a life of meaning and purpose.

How do you discover your purpose? You cannot merely adopt someone else's purpose and follow your True North. You can be inspired by others' sense of purpose and work with others to pursue common goals, but ultimately, your purpose is unique to you.

We will be going on a journey through your past, present, and future to visit the times when you were most operating from your purpose. The outcome will be the discovery of words that paint a picture of your unique gift to the world (your purpose). The words you generate should be both intimidating and exciting, while providing you with an inner wisdom to make critical decisions.

Also, we will help you discover how your purpose as a leader aligns with the larger purpose of the organizations you devote your time and energy to.

REDISCOVERING YOUR PURPOSE

What if your deeper purpose as a leader has been staring back at you all this time waiting for you to discover it?

After working with thousands of participants in programs around the world, we can comfortably say that the challenge isn't to *find* your purpose; rather, it's to rediscover and own the purpose that has always been there. Your unique purpose is so essential to who you are that you have most likely been too close to it to see it. The good news is that your purpose has shown up many times in your life. What we want to do now is give you the perspective and distance needed to say, "I see you now."

There are three areas of your life journey that can help you to rediscover your purpose. The first two listed below are related to your passions. Where there is passion, purpose is usually nearby:

I. Magical moments that you experienced as a kid when you were lost in the pure joy of an activity before the world told you who or what you should or shouldn't be.

II. Things you love to do that will always be a part of who you are (skiing, singing, etc.)

III. The third area is related to your crucibles—times in your life when everything else is stripped away and your purpose reveals itself.

We have also included prompts that either help fill in the gaps or in some cases are the tipping point to rediscovering your purpose. Remember we are looking for the patterns over time that are an expression of your purpose.

EXERCISE 10.1: REDISCOVERING YOUR PASSION AND PURPOSE

This exercise will draw on your life story work in Part One of this fieldbook.

First, review your life story, then answer the following questions:

When you were a child, what did you most love doing?

_____

_____

_____

_____

Describe one of those moments.

_____

_____

_____

_____

What elements are central to the story?

_____

_____

_____

_____

How did you feel in that moment?

_____

_____

_____

_____

When you were a teenager, what brought you the most joy and satisfaction—especially when things were challenging? Describe a particular moment, including how you felt and what was happening.

_____

_____

_____

_____

What unique or special talent did influential mentor(s) in your life see in you (i.e., why did they invest their time and energy in you)?

_____

_____

_____

_____

If you had no limitations on your life—no concerns about money, family obligations, or work requirements—how would you spend your time and energy?

_____

_____

_____

_____

What can you learn from your crucible stories that might relate to your purpose?

_____

_____

_____

_____

What is something you have been passionate about for an extended period of time in your life (e.g., playing the violin, sailing, painting, etc.)? How do you feel when you are doing it?

_____

_____

_____

_____

In the last year, describe your most enjoyable, satisfying, and energizing moment. What happened and how did it make you feel?

_____

_____

_____

_____

EXERCISE 10.2: DEFINING YOUR PURPOSE

Our hope is that as you answered the questions in exercise 10.1 you smiled a couple of times as you recalled moments when you were operating from your purpose.

Our goal in this section is to identify a unique set of words that help you access your purpose as a leader. The words you discover are like a combination that opens a safe. The combination isn't what is inside (living your purpose), but it is the means by which you access your purpose.

Before you define your purpose, we need to clarify a number of misperceptions of what purpose is not.

Purpose is not:

A. **A job, role, or title that you find exciting**
Example: Lead IBM's new markets department to achieve exceptional business results
What happens when this person leaves IBM or changes careers? If you can be fired from it, it's not your purpose.

B. **A cause**
Example: Help to end hunger around the world
Yes, this is a powerful cause and one that all of us should help make happen, but how do you live this purpose with your kids or friends? If you can turn it off, it's not your purpose. It may be a strategy by which you express your purpose, but your purpose sits underneath that beautiful cause. Your purpose operates in all parts of your life.

C. **A string of words that serves to cover all the bases**
Example: Be a driver in the infrastructure business that allows each person to achieve their needed outcomes while also mastering the new drivers of our business as I balance my family and work demands
If it sounds like an insurance policy, then it's not your purpose.

D. **All the right words**
Example: Continually and consistently develop and facilitate the growth and development of myself and others leading to great performance.
If HR loves your purpose, it's probably not your purpose.

A good purpose will:

- Work in all parts of your life. Your friends and spouse would all say, "That is really you."
- Make you smile as in the end, it is really you at your best, and how you want to be remembered.
- Has unique language from your life journey that speaks to you
- Each word has significant meaning

Here are some examples of purpose statements that have achieve the above:

- To catalyze people who fly a kite to imagine the rocket
- With tenacity, create brilliance
- To always be the lead violinist in the orchestra of life
- To be the inquisitive shit stirrer that helps you step into your deeper wisdom
- Find the elephant and ride it out of the room
- To be the behind the scenes gentle kick in the ass reason for success
- To be the wuxia master who saves the kingdom
- To never chooses the half-truth when the whole truth can be one

Our article "From Purpose to Impact" from the May 2014 issue of *Harvard Business Review* has good examples and stories that may help as you begin to think about your own purpose.

Finally, don't worry about, "What will others think if they hear these crazy words of mine?" Let's get it to sing for you, and then we can worry about how you package it for the world. As Oliver Wendell Holmes so poignantly wrote: "Most of us go to our graves with our music still inside us, unplayed."

Time to hear the music.

Step 1: Using your answers from exercise 10.1 as raw material, write down elements of your purpose in the space below. Do not worry about complete sentences; just make a list of thoughts, impressions, and words that speak to you.

_____

_____

_____

_____

_____

_____

_____

Step 2: Now summarize those elements uncovered in Step 1 into one, single, declarative statement in the following form:

"My leadership purpose is _____ !" (fill in the blank as your first rough DRAFT purpose statement).

_____

_____

_____

_____

_____

_____

_____

Step 3: How would you describe your purpose to a 10-year-old?

_____

_____

_____

_____

_____

_____

_____

Step 4: What is it about the purpose phrases above that describe your unique gift?

_____

_____

_____

Step 5: Taking the words that best capture your unique purpose, once again complete the following sentence: My leadership purpose is:

LEADING WITH PURPOSE

The more consistent your actions are with your purpose, the more authentic you are as a leader. In other words, once you embrace your purpose, you can bring that purpose to your leadership.

> This is the true joy in life, the being used for a purpose recognized by yourself as a mighty one; the being thoroughly worn out before you are thrown on the trash heap; the being a force of Nature instead of a feverish, selfish little clod of ailments and grievances complaining that the world will not devote itself to making you happy.
>
> —George Bernard Shaw, preface to *Man and Superman*

EXERCISE 10.3: LIVING YOUR PURPOSE

Using the purpose statement you crafted in the previous exercise, make a list of situations or moments when you were fully living your purpose. Include everything you can think of from the past to the present, even if the event or situation lasted for only a short time.

When in the past have you been operating from your leadership purpose?

_____

_____

_____

_____

Where in your life today are you operating from your leadership purpose?

_____

_____

_____

_____

List some examples of situations in the future that might enable you to fulfill the purpose of your leadership.

1. _____

2. _____

3. _____

What are you going to change today so that tomorrow you are better aligned with your purpose?

_____

_____

_____

_____

ALIGNMENT OF INDIVIDUAL AND ORGANIZATIONAL PURPOSE

We now look at the alignment between your purpose as a leader and the organizations where you contribute your time (school, job, volunteer work). Every organization has a purpose, whether it is a company that makes life-saving drugs or a grocery store chain. Having a clear sense of the connection between you and the organization is one of the key steps to owning how you express your leadership purpose over time. Now let's help you make the connection.

What is the purpose of the organization you are currently working for or involved with?

_____

_____

_____

_____

How does the organization's purpose connect to your purpose as a leader?

_____

_____

_____

_____

What part of what you do within the organization is most aligned with your purpose?

_____

_____

_____

_____

What can you do to increase the alignment of your purpose and that of your organization?

_____

_____

_____

_____

A LIFE OF PURPOSEFUL LEADERSHIP

In this chapter, you have looked through the lens of your life story to discover your passions and the purpose of your leadership.

Now that you have articulated your purpose, you will be a better leader because you know why you are leading. With this clarity of purpose, you can find others who share your passions thus building a community or team and multiplying the impact of your actions. In the next chapter, we turn to empowering other people to step up and lead by inspiring and aligning them with a common purpose.

KEY TAKEAWAYS

- To become an authentic leader, it is essential that you understand the purpose of your leadership.

- By examining your life story and your crucibles, you can uncover your unique gift as a leader and thus discover the purpose of your leadership.

- Living your purpose enables you to empower others to step up and lead.

- Aligning your purpose with your organization's purpose helps to maximize the impact of your leadership.

SUGGESTED READING

Craig, N. and Snook, S. "From Purpose to Impact," *Harvard Business Review*, May 2014.

Frankl, V. *Man's Search for Meaning*. Boston: Beacon Press, 2006.

Hurst, A. *The Purpose Economy: How Your Desire for Impact, Personal Growth and Community Is Changing the World*. Boise, ID: Elevate; Gold edition, 2014.

Ibarra, H., Ely, R., and Kolb, D. "Women Rising: The Unseen Barriers," *Harvard Business Review*, September 2013.

O'Kelly, E. *Chasing Daylight: How My Forthcoming Death Transformed My Life*. New York: McGraw Hill 2008.

Pink, D. *Drive*. New York, NY: Riverhead books 2011.

Seligman, M. *Flourish: A Visionary New Understanding of Happiness and Well-being*. New York, NY: Atria Books 2011.

11

Empower Others to Lead

> As we look ahead into the next century,
> leaders will be those who empower others.
> —*Bill Gates*

Authentic leaders expect outstanding performance from themselves, from others, and from their teams in order to achieve outstanding results. But high expectations and high standards are not enough to achieve these results. There must also be a climate in which others are empowered to lead and to assume responsibility for achieving the organization's goals and objectives. Authentic leaders empower others in their organization by aligning them around a common purpose and set of values and encouraging them to step up and lead. Thus they create organizations of empowered leaders at all levels.

EMPOWERMENT

By empowering leaders throughout their organizations, authentic leaders create high-performance organizations because all members are encouraged and inspired to reach their full potential. First, you must be an authentic leader yourself, and then foster a climate of mutual respect by treating people as equals, listening to them, and learning from them. To do so, you must be genuine in your interactions and encourage openness and authenticity in conversations. You must expect—not just endure—debate and constructive criticism as you empower your teammates.

Being an authentic leader requires you to have those hard conversations that give others the knowledge, courage, and confidence to step up and lead. Empowered leaders will continue to step up because they have the confidence that they will be supported, even if things do not work out well. As an empowering leader, you must help others recognize their unique gifts while also creating an environment that rewards those gifts in action.

Thus you create a climate in which others around you are comfortable engaging in authentic conversations and assuming responsibility to lead. When you give other leaders the respect and responsibility to lead and create a climate of trust, they will feel accountable for results and willing to align their actions around a shared sense of purpose.

Empowerment Comes *with* Responsibility

Early in my time at Medtronic, I made a point of talking a great deal about empowerment. Yet when I challenged people's plans and asked why they were not meeting their performance commitments, I received feedback that my questions and challenges were not empowering.

I thought hard about this, wondering what was required to get people to *take* responsibility for meeting their goals rather than *resisting* accountability. It turned out to be a matter of engaging them in authentic conversations. At a management meeting, I explained that an integral component of empowerment was taking accountability for achieving results. In the end, one of my critics said, "Now we understand you better. You're talking about empowerment *with* responsibility." The words were the same, but now there was a shared understanding of what those words meant and an acceptance of the importance of being held accountable for outcomes, not just effort.

—Bill George

EXERCISE 11.1: WHAT HAVE YOU LEARNED ABOUT EMPOWERMENT?

The purpose of this exercise is to learn from your experiences of being empowered and of empowering others. To answer the next questions, think about the best leaders you have either worked for or observed closely in your life.

What did these leaders communicate about your potential to lead?

_____

_____

_____

_____

When you did not perform well, what did they say or do?

_____

_____

_____

_____

What impact did they have on you?

_____

_____

_____

_____

Now let's turn to situations where you successfully empowered others.

Describe a time when you successfully empowered others.

_____

_____

_____

_____

What did you do that others found to be empowering? What were the outcomes?

_____

_____

_____

_____

Describe a situation when you were not effective at empowering others.

_____

_____

_____

_____

What prevented you from empowering others?

_____

_____

_____

_____

Knowing what you know now, what would you do differently in a similar situation?

_____

_____

_____

_____

FIVE WAYS TO BUILD TRUST AND MUTUAL RESPECT

Empowerment only happens when relationships are based on trust and mutual respect. We learned through our research that authentic leaders use several approaches to build trust and create deep, engaging relationships based on mutual respect. This section introduces you to five of these approaches:

1. Treat others as equals.
2. Listen actively.
3. Learn from people.
4. Share life stories.
5. Align around mission.

In the following exercises you will learn how to put each of these approaches into practice.

Treat Others As Equals

One of the most effective ways to create deeper levels of trust and honesty is to break down hierarchy. Leaders are often afforded higher status and power. As a result, to build relationships based on *mutual* respect (versus authority), it is the leader's responsibility to level the playing field. Seemingly trivial practices can go a long way to help put others at ease when you are in a position of power or authority.

When leading, here are just a few things you might consider to help others feel like they are truly in a relationship based on mutual respect:

- Where do you meet them? Your office or theirs?
- What do you wear when interacting with them (how formal)?
- Where do you sit at meetings (at the head or sides)?
- Who arrives first?
- Where do you eat your meals?
- What salutations do you use in correspondence/e-mails?

EXERCISE 11.2: LEVEL THE PLAYING FIELD

The goal of this exercise is to help you become more aware of inherent power and status differentials often associated with leading.

Think of leaders you've worked for (or observed closely) who were *effective* at leveling the playing field, in spite of obvious differences in formal authority or position.

What did they do to make others feel like they were valued and respected?

_____

_____

_____

_____

Think of leaders you've worked for (or observed closely) who were *ineffective* at leveling the playing field.

What did they do to remind others that this relationship was not *one based on mutual respect?*

_____

_____

_____

_____

Listen Actively

Perhaps the single most powerful gift we can offer someone is our undivided attention. From the time we are born, we just want to be seen, to be heard. The simple act of listening sends a powerful message that we care. Active listening is a sign of respect.

The bad news? Most of us are not very good listeners. The good news? Active listening is a skill that can be learned. The best news? When mastered, the simple act of being present and listening can be an incredibly powerful tool for creating trust and mutual respect.

EXERCISE 11.3: ACTIVE LISTENING

How good are you at listening? I mean really listening? Paying attention is hard work! Apparently, it costs us to "pay" attention. Our minds naturally wander. We are busy. Our smartphones are pinging; music is playing; screens are flashing. We live in an auditorily and visually loud world. We are easily distracted.

Go to any restaurant, movie theater, meeting, or classroom. Look around. What do you see? People gathered together supposedly to share a meal, watch entertainment, discuss a business topic, or learn. And yet, if you look closely, how many are fully listening to each other? Active listening is not simply hearing, and it's definitely not selective listening, passive listening, or multitasking. Active listening requires a personal commitment to be fully present, listen deeply, empathize, and learn something.

If you want to become a better active listener, three things must happen. First, you have to decide that it's important (commitment). Second, become more aware of what is going on in your head (self-monitoring). Third, practice, practice, practice (ask for feedback).

These exercises will help you get started.

Commitment

Think of someone who is a really good listener. How do they make you feel?

_____

_____

_____

_____

Self-Monitor

The next time you talk to someone, pay close attention to your mind chatter. How present are you? Where are your eyes? What are you thinking as this person is talking?

_____

_____

_____

_____

Practice

The next time you talk to someone, try the following:

- *STOP talking, don't interrupt, don't judge, don't problem-solve, don't prepare your response.*
- *DO face the speaker, lean forward, make eye contact, nod, watch their nonverbals (and yours).*
- *PAUSE (use silence) . . . and then: Label emotions (e.g. You sound . . . You seem . . .), paraphrase (e.g., Are you saying? What I heard is . . .), ask clarifying questions, and summarize.*

  And then ask them for some feedback. How did you do? What did you learn?

_____

_____

_____

_____

Learn from People

When someone says, "Hey, I could really use your advice on this issue," or "Can you help me understand how this works?" how does that make you feel? When others value our experience, opinion, or expertise, we feel respected. The simple act of ending a conversation or meeting by saying, "Hey, this was all very helpful. I learned a great deal from you today" goes a long way toward empowering others and building a relationship based on mutual respect.

EXERCISE 11.4: ADVOCACY AND INQUIRY

"Seek first to understand; and then to be understood." This popular saying is widely attributed to Saint Francis and more recently popularized by Stephen Covey. No matter the source, the message is clear: If we truly want to learn from others, we need to fight our natural tendency to weight advocacy over inquiry.

If your primary goal in a conversation is to state your case, look good, and/or win the argument, you are definitely not in a learning mode. The simplest way to move a conversation forward is to ask a question. "Can you help me understand your thinking here?" Striking the right balance of advocacy and inquiry lies at the heart of effective communication and having an effective conversation built on mutual respect.

Most of us aren't aware of how easily we slip into the mode of promoting our own views (advocacy over inquiry). The next time you are in a meeting or having a conversation with someone, ask a third party to monitor how well you balance advocacy and inquiry by coding your "air time" in the following way:

What percentage of time were you advocating your position? (Include quotes/examples of how you were advocating.)

_____

_____

_____

_____

What percentage of time were inquiring about the other's position? (Include quotes/examples of how you were inquiring.)

_____

_____

_____

_____

Share Life Stories

One of the most effective ways to break down barriers and create a deeper level of trust and honesty is to talk about the challenging experiences you have faced, the times when you have made mistakes or failed, and how you learned from them. By admitting your mistakes and explaining what you learned from them, you give others permission to do the same.

EXERCISE 11.5: SHARING YOUR STORY

The goal of this exercise is to share a personal story with someone else. Sharing your story builds meaningful connections and may encourage others to share their stories as well.

Think of a story about yourself that you are not particularly proud of, a time when you made a mistake or learned a difficult lesson. Share your story with a close colleague or friend. After you have finished, ask this person to share a story with you.

What did you learn from this experience? About yourself? About the other person?

_____

_____

_____

_____

Align around Mission

If you are going to inspire others to take on difficult challenges, it is important to help them understand their purpose. In so doing, you can empower them to live it through their actions.

EXERCISE 11.6: EMPOWERING OTHERS TO FULFILL THEIR PURPOSE

The goal of this exercise is to discover ways you can help others understand their purpose and encourage them to realize it. Begin this exercise by talking with a few friends or colleagues about their passions and the purpose of their leadership.

How did you help them by having this conversation?

_____

_____

_____

_____

One of the greatest challenges leaders have is to align the people on their team or in their organization around a common purpose that is consistent with the overall mission of the organization. One of the ways to improve alignment is by sharing why you think the organization's purpose and values are meaningful to you, and explaining how they fit with your purpose and values. Then invite others to do the same.

Engaging others around you in conversations about purpose and values can inspire your entire team to fulfill the organization's purpose. Your teammates will become more committed to living by those values. In the twenty-first century, the saying "people support what they help create" is truer than ever.

EXERCISE 11.7: ALIGNING OTHERS AROUND A SHARED PURPOSE

The purpose of this exercise is to explore how you can align people around a common purpose. Your challenge is to help those around you connect their purpose and values with the purpose and values of your team or organization.

What is the connection between your purpose and the purpose of your organization? If you are currently not on a team or in an organization, think of a time when you were and assess the alignment between your personal passions and purpose and those of your organization.

_____

_____

_____

_____

_____

_____

How have you been able in the past to inspire others around a common purpose and set of values?

_____

_____

_____

_____

_____

_____

What specific steps will you take to create alignment in your organization around shared purpose and values?

_____

_____

_____

_____

_____

_____

Meeting Commitments by Empowering Others

It is not at all uncommon for leaders to feel squeezed between meeting performance goals and empowering others. When leaders feel that performance goals are slipping from their grasp, they are tempted to seize control from the very people they are working to empower. Yet often the problems in meeting performance goals result from too little empowering of others, not too much. It is therefore crucial that you use empowerment as a vehicle to meet your goals.

There will be times when it is both necessary and appropriate to step in, make tough choices, and direct the actions of others. When you intervene with honesty and out of necessity, you can maintain a culture of empowerment. But if you seize control from others reflexively and out of fear, you risk destroying the very trust and confidence required to engage others.

EXERCISE 11.8: HOW CAN I EMPOWER OTHERS AND STILL MEET PERFORMANCE GOALS?

This exercise explores strategies for managing yourself when you perceive a conflict between empowering others and achieving performance goals.

Briefly describe a situation in which you faced a conflict between empowering other people and reaching your performance goals.

_____

_____

_____

_____

How did you resolve the conflict?

_____

_____

_____

_____

How can you empower others and still reach your goals when sensing a conflict?

_____

_____

_____

_____

If you are currently in a leadership position, what will you do in the next month to empower the important people in your professional life to be more effective as leaders?

Your direct reports:

_____

_____

_____

_____

Your peers:

_____

_____

_____

_____

Your superiors:

_____

_____

_____

_____

EMPOWERING OTHERS TO LEAD

Each of the approaches described in this chapter helps you empower others to step up and lead. Make a point of experimenting with those suggestions that initially seem least risky to you. By so doing, you will learn the best ways you can empower leaders around you.

Empowerment comes in many flavors. Some authentic leaders are master orators, ready to come on stage and give a rousing speech to their troops. Others are adept listeners who provide support and a sounding board for their people. Still others develop every member of their team in ways that fit each individual. Regardless of the style they employ, effective leaders ensure that they empower others in authentic ways and foster genuine interactions among them.

In the next section, we explore this fundamental question of style when it comes to leading.

LEADERSHIP STYLE—A CONTINGENCY APPROACH

Style is simply how you lead. There is no one best style for leading. This is good news, because we are all incredibly different! However, some styles are better than others; it all depends.

What should it depend on? At any given moment, your leadership style should be influenced by two fundamental factors: first, who you are, and second, the relevant variables in the situation. This entire workbook is designed to help you gain some clarity surrounding the first variable. We all have a modal style of leading. All other things being equal, this is the style that comes most naturally to you, given who you are—your core values, your passions, your capabilities, and your purpose. The developmental path to improve on the first variable is self-awareness.

The developmental capacity that works in support of the second variable is situational awareness. By periodically placing yourself in various leadership and organizational contexts—often referred to as *stretch assignments*—you increase your ability to read and respond to a wide range of potentially relevant variables in the situation. Such variables might include societal norms, organizational culture, subordinate needs, task demands, industry dynamics, time pressure, and generational patterns.

For example, what worked for your grandparents' generation might not work for you. In only two generations the dominant style of leading (and parenting) has gone from a largely top-down, hierarchal, control approach to leading (children should be seen and not heard; employees too), to a much more distributed and empowering approach to influence (hence, the title of this chapter). Still, what might work with software engineers in Silicon Valley might not work with platinum miners in South Africa. Even within the same company, what's effective on the shop floor might not be effective in the R&D lab. Potentially relevant situational variables range across all levels of analysis, from the macrogenerational/societal, all the way down to the individual/task. For example, what works to motivate Scott on most days might be a fairly light touch; however, if it's his first time on a task, a more structured approach might work better.

The following list summarizes six core leadership styles. Review it to see if you can recognize your modal style or the one with which you feel most comfortable.

Six Core Leadership Styles

- **Directive** leadership demands immediate compliance.
- **Engaged** leadership mobilizes people toward a vision.
- **Coaching** leadership develops people for the future.
- **Consensus** leadership builds buy-in through participation.
- **Affiliative** leadership creates emotional bonds and harmony.
- **Expert** leadership expects excellence and self-direction.

EXERCISE 11.9: YOUR NATURAL STYLE OF LEADING

As you review your entire history of leading—whether in formal positions of authority or informal situations when you simply stepped up and attempted to influence others toward some collective goal—how would you describe your most common style of leading? Or all other things being equal, what is your natural style of leading? Select one name from the list of core styles above.

Natural style of leading:

EXERCISE 11.10: YOUR PREFFERED STYLE OF BEING LED

We all have a natural style when it comes to leading. We also have a preferred style of being led. These two may or may not be the same.

Reflect on your lifetime of experience as a follower. Selecting from the list above, what is your preferred style of being led?

Preferred style of being led:

_____

EXERCISE 11.11: MOST EFFECTIVE STYLE OF LEADING

Think of an example where *you* successfully influenced others toward a collective goal, perhaps one where you raised their game to another level. This could be a situation where you were in a formal position of authority or a time when you simply stepped up and led. Drawing from the list of core styles above, how would you describe your leadership style in that situation?

Style when at your best:

_____

_____

Describe what you think were the most relevant variables in that situation:

_____

_____

_____

_____

EXERCISE 11.12: MOST EFFECTIVE STYLE OF BEING LED

Now think of an example where someone else successfully influenced you toward a collective goal, perhaps one that raised your game to another level, got the most out of you. Drawing from the list of core styles above, how would you describe the leadership style in that situation?

Style that got the most out of you: _____ ____

Describe what you think were the most relevant variables in that situation:

_____

_____

_____

_____

EXERCISE 11.13: LEADERSHIP STYLE INVENTORY

Review your answers to exercises 11.9–11.12. Are the four styles—natural style of leading, preferred style of being led, most effective style of leading, and most effective style of being led—all the same? Adding situational context to the mix, summarize your understanding of how to think about leadership style:

_____

_____

_____

_____

_____

_____

_____

_____

LEADERSHIP STYLE—A DEVELOPMENTAL APPROACH

When it comes to style, effectiveness is a function of fit. Given who you are and the relevant variables in the situation, to the extent that you can "flex your style" to fit the situation and still be authentic, you will be successful. Put differently, you can be effective applying any of the six core styles listed above as long as the style you select matches the situation *and* you can apply it in a manner that is authentic to who you are.

We all have natural or modal styles of leading. Therefore, who we are places some very real limits as to how far we can flex—or adapt our styles—to fit the demands of any given situation. For example, if you face a challenge where you have very little time and your natural style is to lead by consensus, adopting a more directive style might be necessary. However, the manner in which you apply this style has to remain authentic to who you are.

From a purely stylistic perspective, there are at least three ways to increase the likelihood that you will be effective as a leader over time. First, try to select a general context that fits your natural or modal style of leading, most of the time. Second, continue to work on becoming more self-aware. And third, remain open to the infinite number of potentially relevant variables in the situation. From a developmental perspective, to the extent that you can increase self-awareness and situational awareness over time, you can increase the range of situations within which you can be effective. This is a lifelong process.

KEY TAKEAWAYS

- Authentic leaders empower others to lead.
- To empower others, we must create a culture of authenticity, high standards, and shared responsibility through leading by example.
- To be an empowering leader, we must have honest conversations that build trust and engagement in our team or organization.
- Authentic leaders treat everyone as equals, listen actively, learn from others, share their stories, and align people around a shared purpose.
- Leadership style is simply how we lead.

- There is no one best style of leading, but some styles are better than others. It all depends.
- Leadership effectiveness is a function of the fit between who we are, the relevant variables in the situation, and our style.
- We can be effective applying any of the six core styles of leading as long as they fit the situation *and* we apply them in a way that is true to our authentic self.
- To the extent that we improve our self-awareness and situational awareness, over time we can increase the range of situations in which you can be effective.

SUGGESTED READING

Batstone, D. *Saving the Corporate Soul*. San Francisco: Jossey-Bass, 2003.

Bossidy, L., and Charan, R. *Execution*. New York: Crown Business, 2002.

Bower, J. *The CEO Within*. Boston: Harvard Business School Press, 2007.

Collins, J., and Porras, J. *Built to Last*. New York: HarperCollins, 1994.

De Pree, M. *Leadership Is an Art*. New York: Doubleday, 1990.

Ferrazzi, K. *Never Eat Alone*. New York: Doubleday, 2005.

Heifetz, R., and Linsky, M. *Leadership on the Line*. Boston: Harvard Business School Press, 2002.

Kanter, R. M. *Confidence*. New York: Crown Business, 2004.

Lawrence, P., and Nohria, N. *Driven*. San Francisco: Jossey-Bass, 2002.

McGregor, D. *The Human Side of Enterprise*. New York: McGraw-Hill, 1960.

Pfeffer, J. *Managing with Power*. Boston: Harvard Business School Press, 1992.

Senge, P. M., Kleiner, A., Roberts, C., Ross, R. B., and Smith, B. J. *The Fifth Discipline Field Book*. New York: Currency Book, 1994.

Sutton, R. *The No Asshole Rule*. New York: Business Plus, 2007.

Torbert, W. R. *Action Inquiry: The Secret of Timely and Transforming Leadership*. San Francisco: Berrett-Koehler, 2004.

Useem, M. *Leading Up*. New York: Crown Business, 2001.

Whitehead, J. *A Life in Leadership*. New York: Basic, 2005.

12

Become a Global Authentic Leader

> "In Globalization 1.0, which began around 1492, the world went from size
> large to size medium. In Globalization 2.0, the era that introduced us to
> multinational companies, it went from size medium to size small.
> And then around 2000 came Globalization 3.0, in which the
> world went from being small to tiny."
> —*Thomas Friedman*, The World is Flat

How to follow your True North and be an authentic leader across a wide variety of cultural and geographic differences is the focus of this chapter. In today's world we believe that those leaders who excel in a global context will participate in defining how organizations operate in the twenty-first century.

All that you have learned so far in each chapter is critical to your ability to be a global authentic leader. Your leadership purpose, core values, and sweet spot form the solid foundation that allows you to traverse the world beyond where you grew up. In running programs across the globe, we have found that when people from very different cultures tell their crucible stories, the world goes from small to very, *very* tiny.

Yet each of us has a set of cultural norms and beliefs we grew up with that shapes how we see the world and interpret others' actions. As we discussed in the values chapter, *integrity* can assume different—and even contradictory—meanings, depending upon one's cultural origins. Our goal in this chapter is to help you clarify your existing worldview, as well as discover the additional experiences that could support your continuing journey as a global authentic leader.

To this point, we will focus on helping you with three key attributes of demonstrating global intelligence that are integral to authentic leadership. We began to work on these in Chapter 4 on self-awareness. Now we bring these to the level of working in a global environment.

   A. *Awareness:* How aware are you of the alignment of your True North with the cultural norms of others from across the globe?

      Are you clear enough about who you are to comfortably operate in a culture very different from the one you are used to?

      How well can you operate as a minority with little or no understanding of the deep historical context that drives the beliefs and behaviors of others around you?

   B. *Curiosity:* How much are you willing to be curious about others' ways of operating in the world?

      Are you willing to see how doing things differently—as long as they are consistent with your values—may actually work better in a given cultural context?

      How is your curiosity impacted when cultural differences create tension and lack of trust?

   C. *Empathy:* How well are you truly able to see the world from someone else's perspective, especially when he or she is from a very different culture?

      Are you able to get beyond the transactional demands of day-to-day activities to see the world from a very different view than yours?

      How well can you help people from another culture feel that they are not alone?

ACCESSING YOUR GLOBAL INSIGHTS

EXERCISE 12.1: YOUR GLOBAL LEARNING JOURNEY

We want you to begin to understand how well you have started the journey to become a global authentic leader. Even if you have never left your native country, you have interacted with and experienced people from other cultures. All the lessons are there for you to uncover, so let's begin.

Reviewing your life story, describe your most impactful experiences traveling, interacting with people from other cultural backgrounds in your life, or living/studying/working outside your native country.

Experience 1:

_____

_____

_____

_____

_____

_____

_____

_____

Experience 2:

_____

_____

_____

_____

_____

_____

_____

_____

Experience 3:

_____

_____

_____

_____

_____

_____

_____

_____

Experience 4:

_____

_____

_____

_____

_____

_____

_____

AWARENESS, CURIOSITY, AND EMPATHY

Let's now begin to strengthen your levels of awareness, curiosity, and empathy. Each of these experiences contains a deep level of information for you to learn from.

Awareness is not something that just happens to you. Becoming aware of how you function and are similar to/different from others requires intentional moments of reflection.

EXERCISE 12.2: DEEPENING YOUR AWARENESS

In this exercise we want to help you to expand on your level of awareness in terms of how you have experienced yourself in other cultures.

What stands out in terms of what you learned from the four global experiences?

_____

_____

_____

_____

_____

_____

What surprised you about your reactions to differences in the people and their culture?

_____

_____

_____

_____

_____

_____

How did these experiences help you identify potential biases/blind spots in terms of how you think things "should" be done when operating in another culture?

_____

_____

_____

_____

_____

_____

What did you learn about yourself and who you are from these experiences that couldn't be learned in any other way?

_____

_____

_____

_____

_____

_____

What has been the impact of moments when your cultural bias dominated your behavior with those from another culture?

_____

_____

_____

_____

_____

_____

What steps can you take to maximize your ability to operate from a place of global awareness in the future?

_____

_____

_____

_____

_____

_____

EXERCISE 12.3: CURIOSITY

In this exercise we want to help you expand on your level of curiosity in terms of how you experience yourself in other cultures.

In what ways did your global experiences stimulate your cultural curiosity, your passion for diverse experiences, and your desire to learn more about new cultures?

_____

_____

_____

_____

_____

_____

What is your greatest insight and lesson from being curious about how others live and think in their culture?

_____

_____

_____

_____

_____

_____

What has been the impact of moments when you were not curious about other people and their cultures?

_____

_____

_____

_____

_____

_____

What steps can you take to maximize your ability to operate from a place of global curiosity in the future?

_____

_____

_____

_____

_____

EXERCISE 12.4: EMPATHY

In this exercise we want you to look at how you have accessed empathy in the past and to discover ways to leverage that ability in the future.

First let's look at times when others didn't have empathy for you.

When did you feel alone and misunderstood in another culture or context?

_____

_____

_____

_____

_____

What impact did this experience have on you?

_____

_____

_____

_____

_____

_____

Now let's look at your global experiences and where you demonstrated empathy.

How have your global experiences helped you to have empathy for others?

_____

_____

_____

_____

_____

_____

What is your greatest insight and lesson from these moments of empathy?

_____

_____

_____

_____

_____

_____

What has been the impact of moments when you did not have empathy for those you were engaged with from other cultures?

_____

_____

_____

_____

_____

_____

What steps can you take to maximize your ability to operate from a place of global empathy in the future?

_____

_____

_____

_____

_____

_____

EXERCISE 12.5: AREAS FOR FUTURE DEVELOPMENT

With which cultures do you feel you have deep levels of awareness, curiosity, and empathy based on your life experiences so far?

_____

_____

_____

_____

_____

_____

With which cultures would you like to have deeper levels of awareness, curiosity, and empathy?

_____

_____

_____

_____

_____

Whom do you know from one of those cultures that could help you increase your awareness, curiosity, and empathy?

_____

_____

_____

_____

_____

_____

A LIFE OF GLOBAL LEADERSHIP

In this chapter, you have looked through the lens of your life story to discover who you are as a global authentic leader.

All of us are on a journey of discovery; we will continue to encounter new people and new places in the world. Each person we meet is on a similar journey. Hopefully, we can engage with our fellow travelers from a place of awareness, curiosity, and empathy.

If we are to become truly authentic leaders, we must honor not only our own worldview, but honor those of others as well. Whether our colleagues live across the street or across the globe, this is the mark of authentic leadership.

KEY TAKEAWAYS

- Becoming a global authentic leader is a key opportunity for anyone leading in the twenty-first century.

- What you have learned in earlier chapters from your life story and your crucibles can help you better understand others with very different backgrounds.

- *Awareness* allows us to bridge the differences between us and others so we can all follow our True North.

- *Curiosity* opens us to the possibility of discovering without judgment very different ways of operating and functioning in the world.

- *Empathy* enhances our ability to reach out to others and have them feel a deeper connection as we realize we are not alone as we face different ways of operating in the world.

- Applying the insights from this chapter benefits you beyond just being a global authentic leader. How we interact with others across the table—appreciating awareness of our differences, curiosity about how we think, and empathy in our challenging moments—is fundamental to any leader.

SUGGESTED READING

Hall, E. *Beyond Culture*. New York: Anchor Books, 1976.

Hofstede, G., Hofstede, J. G., and Minkov, M. *Cultures and Organizations: Software of the Mind*, ed. 3. New York: McGraw Hill, 2010.

Livermore, D. *Leading with Cultural intelligence: The Real Secret to Success*, ed. 2. New York: AMACOM, 2015.

Mendenhall, M., Olslan, J., Bird A., Oddou G., Maznevski M., Stevens M., and Stahl G. *Global Leadership 2e: Research, Practice, and Development* (Global HRM). London Routledge, 2012.

Trompenaars, F., and Hampden-Turner, C. *Riding the Waves of Culture: Understanding Diversity in Global Business*, ed. 3. New York: McGraw Hill, 2012.

13

Create Your Personal Leadership Development Plan

> Make no little plans. They have no magic to stir men's blood
> and probably will not themselves be realized.
> —*Daniel Hudson Burnham*

There is a legacy that only you have the potential to fulfill.

Having completed the exercises in this journey to discover your authentic leadership, you are now ready to put them all together and create *your* own personal leadership development plan (PLDP). Your PLDP is the capstone exercise of this fieldbook. It outines the key actions that will guide your development as a leader.

Your PLDP should be a dynamic document that you revisit from time to time to assess the progress you are making in your leadership development. Just as you are constantly learning from your experiences and growing as a leader, so must your PLDP be updated to track your progress to document what you have learned about your leadership, and to uncover new paths you might want to follow.

In this sense, the PLDP is no different from a strategic plan for your organization. The vision and goals are clear, but the details of the strategy to achieve those goals must be updated based on experience and new information that becomes available.

Although your PLDP is the final step in this fieldbook, for you it is just a milestone en route to becoming an authentic leader. You are like an explorer who knows where she wants to go but is constantly incorporating new aspects of the unknown terrain she is traversing. Your map for the journey needs updating to incorporate new discoveries, and your planned route needs adjusting to find ways around the obstacles you have encountered. You constantly refer to your True North and your compass to help you stay on track and to adapt when you sense that you might be veering off course.

The essential thing here is that this is *your* PLDP, not one that has been handed to you by a consultant or a teacher. You own your plan, you know its truth for you, and only you can decide how and when to adapt your plan to stay aligned with your True North.

Although this is the final chapter of this fieldbook, it is not the destination. Discovering your authentic leadership is not an achievement. There is no final state that allows you simply to close the book and move on to other projects. Authentic leadership is the path you are on. It is a lifelong journey. You will always face new tests of your values and motivations. You will face endless opportunities to get sidetracked from your purpose. The more you develop your authentic leadership, the greater the potential distractions, but the more opportunities you will find to deepen your commitment to your True North.

> When the jazz trumpet player Wynton Marsalis—recently named one of America's Best Leaders by *Fortune* magazine—once asked his father what the key was to being a world-class musician, his father said, "You have to do the one thing that no one else does: Practice every day."

Your challenge now is to step up, articulate your vision of your True North, design your development plan, and practice every day!

EXERCISE 13.1: YOUR PERSONAL LEADERSHIP DEVELOPMENT PLAN

As you continue to build your self-awareness, you will find that continuing to develop a healthy mind and body will serve you well. Begin your plan with a foundation for yourself.

YOUR PERSONAL LEADERSHIP DEVELOPMENT PLAN

I. Intellectual Development

Where will I deepen my mind?

1. _____

2. _____

3. _____

Where will I broaden my mind?

1. _____
2. _____
3. _____

What areas will I discover through reading?

1. _____
2. _____
3. _____

What places would I like to live in or visit?

1. _____
2. _____
3. _____

II. Personal Discipline and Stress Management

What will I do to eat more healthfully?

1. _____
2. _____
3. _____

What will I do to get better exercise?

1. _____
2. _____
3. _____

What will I do to develop consistent sleep patterns?

1. _____
2. _____
3. _____

Which practices will I develop to better manage stress?

Practice	Notes
Meditating or sitting quietly	
Running, walking, or working out	
Yoga or similar practice	
Prayer or reflection	
Talking to spouse, friend, or mentor	
Listening to music	
Watching TV or going to movies	
Other:	

III. Crucibles

Review your work on crucibles from Chapter 3.

What key insights from your crucible stories do you need to keep in front of you at all times?

_____

_____

_____

_____

IV. Self-Awareness

Review your work on self-awareness from Chapter 4 and update it here. Take stock of where you are in your journey toward greater self-awareness and self-acceptance.

Based on all the work you've done to this point, list your top five areas for improvement:

1. _____
2. _____
3. _____
4. _____
5. _____

What are some concrete ways you can become more self-aware?

1. _____
2. _____
3. _____
4. _____
5. _____

How comfortable are you with yourself? What can you do to become more self-accepting?

_____

_____

_____

V. Values, Leadership Principles, and Ethical Boundaries

Review your core values, leadership principles, and ethical boundaries, which you worked on in Chapter 5, and update them here. Then rank them in order of importance. Mark those that are inviolate with an asterisk.

What values are most important to me?

Value Name	Value Definition	Rank

What are the principles on which I base my leadership?

Value Name	Leadership Principle

What are the ethical boundaries that will guide my professional life?

1. _____

2. _____

3. _____

4. _____

5. _____

6. _____

VI. Your Motivations

Review your work in Chapter 6 and update your lists of extrinsic and intrinsic motivations and potential traps.

Category	My Extrinsic Motivations	Rank
1. Monetary compensation		
2. Power		
3. Prestigious title		
4. Public recognition		
5. Social status		
6. Competition		
7. Association with prestigious institutions		
8. Other:		
9. Other:		

Category	My Intrinsic Motivations	Rank
1. Engaging in personal growth and development		
2. Doing a good job		
3. Helping others		
4. Leading and organizing others		
5. Being with people I care about		
6. Finding meaning from my efforts		
7. Being true to my beliefs		
8. Making a difference in the world		
10. Influencing others		
11. Other:		
12. Other:		

Category	My Overall Motivations	Rank

Foreseeable Motivational Trap	What I Can Do Tomorrow to Avoid This Trap?

VII. Your Sweet Spot

Continuing with your review of the work you did in Chapter 6, update your lists of leadership strengths, developmental needs, articulation of your sweet spot, and future situations that might enable you to fully operate from your sweet spot.

Your Greatest Leadership Strengths

1. _____

2. _____

3. _____

4. _____

Your Developmental Needs

1. _____

2. _____

3. _____

4. _____

Your Sweet Spot

_____

_____

_____

_____

Future Situations to Find Your Sweet Spot   *Rank*

_____

_____

_____

_____

_____

VIII. Strengthening My Support Team

Review your work in Chapter 7 and update your lists of key people and board of directors.

The most important people in your life are:

1. _____
2. _____
3. _____
4. _____
5. _____

The people with whom you feel you can be completely open are:

1. _____
2. _____
3. _____
4. _____
5. _____

When distressed, you turn to:

1. _____
2. _____
3. _____
4. _____
5. _____

The personal friends who provide you with counsel and advice are:

1. _____
2. _____
3. _____

4. _____

5. _____

Your mentors are:

1. _____

2. _____

3. _____

4. _____

5. _____

Your personal board of directors includes:

1. _____

2. _____

3. _____

4. _____

5. _____

IX. Personal Insights

Review your work in Chapter 8 on having an integrated life and update the practices you will use to keep you grounded and centered.

To be reflective or introspective, you will:

_____

_____

_____

_____

For any mindfulness, spiritual, or religious practice, you will:

_____

_____

_____

_____

To strengthen these practices, you plan to:

_____

_____

_____

_____

If you do not believe in such practices, how do you access a place of peace?

_____

_____

_____

_____

To integrate your personal life, family life, friendships, and community life with your professional life, you plan to do the following:

1. _____

2. _____

3. _____

To achieve your professional and personal goals, you are prepared to make the following sacrifices and trade-offs:

1. _____

2. _____

3. _____

What do you love doing, and how are you going to spend time doing more of it?

_____

_____

_____

_____

X. I to We

Review your work in Chapter 9 and update how you shift from an "I" to "We" orientation.

How will you operate more from a "We" orientation:

_____

_____

_____

_____

XI. Leadership Purpose and Legacy

Review your work in Chapter 10 and update how you apply your purpose as a leader.

The purpose of your leadership is:

_____

_____

_____

_____

Being a leader relates to the whole of your life because:

_____

_____

_____

_____

You would like to leave the following legacy for . . .

Your family:

_____

_____

_____

_____

Your career:

_____

_____

_____

_____

Your friends:

_____

_____

_____

_____

Your community:

_____

_____

_____

_____

At the end of your life, you would like to look back and be able to say:

_____

_____

_____

_____

XII. Leadership Styles

Review your work in Chapter 11 and update how you relate to your leadership styles.

Your preferred leadership style(s) are:

_____

_____

_____

Under pressure, you often revert to the following leadership style:

_____

_____

_____

When dealing directly with very powerful or intimidating people, you:

_____

_____

When exerting power over others, you:

_____

_____

XIII. Developing as a Global Leader

Increasing Your Awareness

The dominant paradigms and biases from your country of origin that you operate within include the following:

1. _____

2. _____

3. _____

To what extent and how do you adapt your mode of operating to accommodate people from different cultural backgrounds?

1. _____

2. _____

3. _____

To understand your blind spots, you use the following ways of getting honest feedback from people of different cultures about how you are seen by them:

1. _____

2. _____

3. _____

Building Your Cultural Curiosity

You are using the following ways to learn from different cultures:

1. _____

2. _____

3. _____

Having Empathy for People in Different Cultures

For you, the difference between having empathy for people in your country of origin and diverse countries that are relatively new to you is:

_____

_____

_____

You are building your empathy for people with distinct cultural differences in the following ways:

1. _____
2. _____
3. _____

XIV. Key Leadership Development Experiences

The key experiences you need in order to further develop your leadership include:

1. _____
2. _____
3. _____
4. _____
5. _____

YOUR TRUE NORTH IS ALIVE

Now that you have completed your development plan, it is time to refine your vision as an authentic leader.

If you want to continue to develop as an authentic leader, you need to balance your past life story with the story of the leader you are becoming. Many leaders stay the same year after year because they have only their past to guide them into the future. Your past, as you have seen, can help you discover your True North. Only your vision of the future can direct you on the rest of the journey. There is a legacy that only you have the potential to fulfill.

EXERCISE 13.2: CREATING YOUR FUTURE

You are going to create a new path for your leadership journey. Take a piece of paper and draw a new path. This path starts at the present and continues into the future.

Looking forward five years into your future, call to mind your wildest dream of what you can become as a leader. Operating fully from your purpose make notes or pictures of the elements of this dream or vision. Ask yourself, "What type of work am I doing? What role do I have? What unique gifts am I exhibiting? What type of impact am I having in my environment? What impact do I have on the people around me? What effect am I having on my organization or company?"

Add other major milestones, events, and changes in the path that need to be included to fill out your vision of the future. Now mark the path where years four, three, two, and one fall, and add any additional milestones or events.

EXERCISE 13.3: YOUR DEVELOPMENT PLAN

The goal of this exercise is to create the action plan to achieve your vision by establishing the next steps.

What is your five-year vision? (Include not just outcomes but what type of leader you will have become.)

_____

_____

_____

_____

_____

_____

Now examine these objectives and consider the next questions.

What would need to be in place in the next two to three years for your five-year vision to become reality?

_____

_____

_____

_____

_____

_____

What will you have to be doing one year from now in order to be on track toward the two- to three-year outcomes?

_____

_____

_____

_____

_____

_____

What must be in place three months from now to be on track for your one-year goals?

_____

_____

_____

_____

_____

What action steps must you begin taking in the next 30 days to meet your three-month goals?

1. _____

2. _____

3. _____

4. _____

5. _____

Congratulations! You have completed your personal leadership development plan, your vision of your leadership five years from now, and laid out the action steps necessary to get you started.

SUGGESTED READING

Kouzes, J., and Posner, B. *The Leadership Challenge.* San Francisco, CA: Jossey-Bass, 2012.

Nohria, N., and Khurana, R. *Handbook of Leadership Theory and Practice.* Boston: Harvard Business School Publishing, 2010.

Afterword

Bill George

> Few will have the greatness to bend history itself. But each of us
> can work to change a small portion of events, and in the total
> of all these acts will be written the history of this generation.
> —*Robert F. Kennedy*

Your True North is in sight. You have the ability, the tools, the motivation, and the passion to get there. If you set your mind to it, you can change the world.

As the late Robert F. Kennedy said, you may not bend history by yourself, but by working with others and stepping up to lead, you can impact the world in important ways that you may not even be able to envision at this point.

Your leadership is needed now. Will you step up to the challenge? Will you empower other leaders to join you in your cause?

Ask yourself these two questions: "If not me, then who? If not now, when?"

When faced with such great challenges, our human tendency is to feel overwhelmed or inadequate. If you feel that way, consider the words of author Marianne Williamson:

> Our deepest fear is not that we are inadequate.
> Our deepest fear is that we are powerful beyond measure. It is our
> light, not our darkness, that most frightens us. We ask ourselves,
> "Who am I to be brilliant, gorgeous, talented, fabulous?" Actually,
> who are you not to be?
> You are a child of God.
> Your playing small does not serve the world. There is nothing
> enlightened about shrinking
> So that other people won't feel insecure around you.

We were born to make manifest the glory of God that is within us. It's not just in some of us. It is in everyone.

—Williamson, M. "Our Greatest Fear," from *A Return to Love*

We all have the gifts of leadership within us. Our calling is to use our gifts to make this world just a little bit better. Do not feel inadequate or modest. Claim your gifts and use them!

Leadership is your choice, not your title.

By pursuing your True North, your calling becomes clear. If you follow your compass, you can become an authentic leader who will change the world and leave behind a legacy to all those who follow in your footsteps.

Appendix A

Ways to Use This Guide

The *Discover Your True North Fieldbook* is designed to enable you to discover your True North. The sequence of chapters is based on the text *Discover Your True North*, which should be read in parallel with this guide. Each chapter in this fieldbook complements *Discover Your True North* and builds on previous chapters in the guide.

The path to becoming an authentic leader is an individual journey. It must start with you, yet you do not need to go on the journey alone. There are several additional ways you can leverage the impact of this fieldbook.

AS AN INDIVIDUAL

As an individual, you can do all the exercises on your own and prepare your personal leadership development plan. The more care you devote to the work, the more it will help you become an authentic and effective leader. Even if someone else magically provided you with the answers to the exercises, they wouldn't be *your* answers, so they wouldn't be authentic. The only journey that matters is the one you choose for yourself.

AS A MEMBER OF A GROUP OF PEERS

Many leaders find it is highly effective to work through this fieldbook with a group of friends or new acquaintances. To increase the impact of this experience, we encourage you to meet on a regular basis with three to six other people to discuss what you are learning. Complete each exercise individually and then meet to discuss your work openly and solicit feedback from other members of your group. Members of the group can take turns leading and facilitating discussions on a rotating basis. Please refer to Appendix B for more information about forming a leadership discussion group.

If you are part of a larger group interested in working together, you may want to work with a designated instructor or professional facilitator, who shapes the content, guides discussions, and keeps the group on track. With larger groups it is still important to use three- to six-person, peer-facilitated discussion groups. Many students in Scott's class at Harvard Business School have said that their leadership discussion groups were among the most important experiences of their two years in the MBA program.

AS A MEMBER OF A TEAM OR AS A TEAM LEADER

If you are the leader of a team in your organization, you may wonder what would happen if all members of your team operated from their True North.

Being part of a team of people working to discover their authentic leadership and helping each other become better leaders by sharing their stories can be a very powerful experience.

You can use this fieldbook with your team at work or in your organization, guiding the team through the process yourself or using a professional team-building consultant. (See Appendix B for ideas about building a structure for your team.)

For further support go to www.authleadership.com.

AS A COACH OR MENTOR

As a coach or mentor, you might use this fieldbook to help emerging leaders through a process of discovering their True North. Each chapter is designed to provide effective preparation for individual sessions. You can provide additional feedback and encouragement, and help emerging leaders explore their stories and insights more deeply to help them access their authenticity.

As a mentor, you will find it essential to have completed each assignment yourself in order to be able to share your insights from your own journey. As a coach, we recommend that you complete the exercises yourself first. To learn more about training coaches, go to www.authleadership.com.

AS A FACILITATOR

The most effective way to create an organizational culture that supports authentic leadership is for a top management team to take the lead. As a facilitator, you are unlikely to participate in the journey on an equal footing with a management team. Yet we recommend that you complete the exercises in this guide yourself in order to fully understand the material and be prepared to work with your client's experiences. For training on this approach and information about how to help leaders become interested in authentic leadership, go to www.authleadership.com.

AS AN EDUCATOR

If you are an educator, you may be asking, "How can I create a course in leadership development for my MBA, executive education, or even undergraduate students?" You can use this fieldbook and *Discover Your True North* as the basis for a course on leadership development. The fieldbook can also complement a course in organizational behavior, managing and leading change, or managing groups and teams.

The fieldbook can be used with leaders at all stages in their careers, whether they are young leaders—including college and graduate students—midcareer leaders and leaders at the top of their organizations, or leaders embarking on the third phase of their leadership journey. The exercises and advice in this fieldbook originated in our experiences teaching groups of executives and MBA students alike to follow their True North and develop as authentic leaders.

We recommend a 12-week course format with three elements each week: (1) an individual assignment from this fieldbook, (2) a six-person leadership discussion group (LDG) session on each assignment, and (3) a plenary class that includes questions and insights from the discussion groups and a case discussion of a leader facing similar issues. We recommend that LDGs be allocated one class period each week. (See Appendix B, Form a Leadership Discussion Group, for suggestions on forming these groups.) If time permits, for three classes per week, the last session could be split into two classes: one to generalize on the LDG discussions, discuss unresolved questions with the entire group, and lecture on the week's concepts, and another to discuss a case.

Appendix B

Form a Leadership Discussion Group

One of the most valuable steps you can take in becoming an authentic leader is to form a leadership discussion group (LDG) that meets on a regular basis to discuss your experiences on your journey to authentic leadership. This fieldbook is set up to be used for LDGs, wherein each group member completes individual assignments prior to group meetings and comes prepared to discuss openly his or her responses with other group members. The LDGs may take one or two weeks per chapter of this guide.

A typical LDG consists of four to eight people who consider themselves to be peers, but not necessarily friends, when they form the group. The key to success lies in all members of the group being open, willing to be vulnerable, and prepared to engage in honest conversation.

To make your group work effectively, it is crucial to establish trust and confidentiality at the outset. All group members must be sincerely interested in growing as leaders themselves and in helping fellow group members grow as well. To preserve the intimacy of the group and ensure that everyone gets adequate airtime, the group should not have more than eight members. It is also important for the group to agree on a meeting place and on the frequency of meetings—preferably a regular schedule of meetings in the same quiet, confidential place to help ensure full attendance. Both weekly and monthly meetings can work well, but in either case, it is essential that all group members commit to being present at every meeting.

The following is a model for a contract that LDG members should discuss and agree on at their first meeting. Modify this contract as necessary so that each group member is happy to sign the contract as an indication of his or her commitment to it.

Leadership Discussion Group Contract

A. Logistics

The LDG will meet each week during [month] on [day of week] from_____to_____. Meetings of the group will be held at_____.

B. Group Leaders

On a rotating basis, one member will be responsible for leading the group each session. The leader is responsible for both planning the program for the meeting and guiding the discussion.

C. Programs

The group should discuss and agree on a way to schedule assignment materials. The material from each session's individual assignments will form the basis for the LDG discussion. The exercises must be completed by each individual in advance, and then shared with the group by each group member. When the exercises in *The Discover Your True North Fieldbook* are complete, the group should determine additional topics it wants to discuss in greater depth, or leave the choice of topic to the facilitator each session.

D. Norms and Expectations

The group should agree in writing on norms relative to: (1) open participation, (2) trust in interaction, (3) confidentiality, and (4) expectations of support. These norms should address the ground rules for respecting differences, setting expectations of tolerance, and for sharing feedback and constructive conflict.

[The following is a set of possible norms that might be discussed by your group and incorporated in whole or in part into your contract.]

1. Openness

To be effective, open sharing with group members is essential to learning. If individuals are not sharing openly with the group, it is the responsibility of group members to raise this with them for discussion within the group. However, it is important that group members not push individuals beyond their comfort zone on personally sensitive matters.

2. Trust

For the LDG to be effective, it is essential that group members trust each member of the group, as well as the group as a whole. Trust is built through honest, open communication and through the expression of care and concern for each other. Members must feel cared for on their journey to becoming effective leaders.

3. Confidentiality

A firm agreement should be reached that nothing said within the group is discussed with others outside the group, even with spouses or partners.

4. Differences

The group should allow for individual differences and make accommodations for each member's goals for the group experience.

5. Tolerance

There are no "right" answers when life priorities or values are discussed, nor should group members make judgments about others in the group.

6. Feedback

Group members offer and receive constructive feedback from each other on their ideas, leadership traits, and communication styles.

7. Challenges

Challenges by other group members are considered to be healthy, if expressed in a respectful manner in which individuals do not engage in personal attacks. If managed well, respectful challenges contribute to meaningful learning for all.

Appendix C

Course Syllabus for Authentic Leadership Development

COURSE PURPOSE

The purpose of authentic leadership development (ALD) is to enable students to develop as leaders of organizations and to embark on paths of personal leadership development. ALD requires personal curiosity and reflection from students, and personal openness and sharing in class discussions, leadership discussion groups, and one-on-one sessions with the professor. Leadership development concepts used in this course will be immediately useful for students and applicable for the rest of their lives.

INTELLECTUAL PREMISE AND COURSE CONCEPTS

The premise of ALD is that leaders who know themselves well and consciously develop their leadership abilities throughout their lifetimes will be more effective and more successful leaders and lead more satisfying and fulfilling lives.

ALD will provide students with many ideas, techniques, and tools to assist in their leadership development journeys, exploring concepts such as lifelong leadership development; leadership crucibles; discovering your authentic self; knowing your principles, values, and ethical boundaries; building support teams; leadership style and power; integrated leadership; and purpose-driven leadership.

BOOK READING

George, B. *Discover Your True North: Becoming an Authentic Leader*. Read this book in its entirety, preferably before the course begins, as we refer to its concepts and its stories throughout the course.

LEADERSHIP DISCUSSION GROUPS (LDGs)

Each class participant will be assigned to a leadership discussion group with five other people. The discussion groups will meet for 90–120 minutes to complete the assignment for the week. These groups enable students to discuss personal materials in a more intimate group setting and to encourage a higher level of openness and reflection than may be possible in the class setting. LDGs will be facilitated by a member of the group, who will be assigned in advance. Each student will have the opportunity to facilitate for two weeks during the course. Facilitators will meet with the professor prior to the LDG and will be asked to submit a summary of the group's discussion after the meeting, including open questions for the full class.

AUTHENTIC LEADERSHIP DEVELOPMENT COURSE PLAN
Week I: Your Life Story

Before the first class, write a one-page paper about why you want to take this course.

Personal assignment: *The Discover Your True North Fieldbook*, Introduction and Chapter 1

Readings: *Discover Your True North*, Introduction and Chapter 1

Class I cases:

Howard Schultz: Building Starbucks Community (A) (HBS Case No.406–127)

Howard Schultz: Building Starbucks Community (B) (HBS Case No. 407–127)

LDG: Discuss *The Discover Your True North Fieldbook*, Introduction and Chapter 1

At the first LDG meeting, begin initially by reviewing Appendix B, Form a Leadership Discussion Group, in *The Discover Your True North Fieldbook* and establishing written guidelines for your group's contract.

Week II: Losing Your Way

Personal assignment: *The Discover Your True North Fieldbook*, Chapter 2

Readings: *Discover Your True North*, Chapter 2

Class II case: Richard Grasso and New York Stock Exchange (HBS Case No. 405–051)

LDG: Discuss *The Discover Your True North Fieldbook*, Chapter 2

Week III: Crucibles

Personal assignment: *The Discover Your True North Fieldbook*, Chapter 3

Readings: *Discover Your True North*, Chapter 3

Bennis, W., and Thomas, R. "Crucibles of Leadership," Harvard Business Review, September 2002

Class III case: Anne Mulcahy: Leading Xerox through the Perfect Storm (A) (HBS Case No. 405–050)

LDG: Discuss *The Discover Your True North Fieldbook*, Chapter 3

Week IV: Self-Awareness

Personal assignment: *The Discover Your True North Fieldbook*, Chapter 4

Readings:

Discover Your True North, Chapter 4

Goleman, D. "What Makes a Leader?" Harvard Business Review, January 2004

Class IV cases:

Kevin Sharer: Sustaining the High-Growth Company (A) (HBS Case No. 406–020)

Kevin Sharer: Sustaining the High-Growth Company (B) (HBS Case No. 409–037)

LDG: Discuss *The Discover Your True North Fieldbook*, Chapter 4

Week V: Values

Personal assignment: *The Discover Your True North Fieldbook*, Chapter 5

Reading: *Discover Your True North*, Chapter 5

Class V case: Narayana Murthy and Compassionate Capitalism (HBS Case No. 406–015)

LDG: Discuss *The Discover Your True North Fieldbook*, Chapter 5

Midterm paper: My Journey to Authentic Leadership

In your midterm paper, which should not exceed 1,500 words, describe the most important experiences in your life to date, including the greatest crucible of your life and how it has impacted your life and your leadership.

Week VI: Sweet Spot

Personal assignment: *The Discover Your True North Fieldbook*, Chapter 6

Reading: *Discover Your True North*, Chapter 6

Class VII case: David Neeleman: Flight Path of a Servant Leader (A) (HBS Case No. 409–024

LDG: Discuss *The Discover Your True North Fieldbook*, Chapter 6

Week VII: Support Team

Personal assignment: *The Discover Your True North Fieldbook*, Chapter 7

Reading: *Discover Your True North*, Chapter 7

Class VIII case: Tad Piper: Crisis at Piper Jaffray (HBS Case No. 406–033)

LDG: Discuss *The Discover Your True North Fieldbook*, Chapter 7

Week VIII: Integrated Life

Personal assignment: *The Discover Your True North Fieldbook*, Chapter 8

Readings: *Discover Your True North*, Chapter 8

LDG: Discuss *The Discover Your True North Fieldbook*, Chapter 8

Class VIII cases:

Martha Goldberg Aronson: Leadership Challenges at Mid-Career (HBS Case No. 406–017)

Philip McCrea: Once an Entrepreneur (A) (HBS Case No. 406–018)

For distribution and discussion in class:

Martha Goldberg Aronson: Leadership Challenges at Mid-Career (HBS Case No. 409–030)

Philip McCrea: Once an Entrepreneur (B) (HBS Case No. 409–025)

Week IX: I to We

Personal assignment: *The Discover Your True North Fieldbook*, Chapter 9

Reading: *Discover Your True North*, Chapter 9

Class IX case: Whole Foods: Balancing Social Mission and Growth (HBS Case 410–023)

LDG: Discuss *The Discover Your True North Fieldbook*, Chapter 9

Week X: Purpose

Personal assignment: *The Discover Your True North Fieldbook*, Chapter 10

Reading: *Discover Your True North*, Chapter 10

Class X case: PepsiCo: Performance with Purpose (HBS Case No. 412–079)

LDG: Discuss *The Discover Your True North Fieldbook*, Chapter 10

Week XI: Empowerment

Personal assignment: *The Discover Your True North Fieldbook*, Chapter 11

Reading: *Discover Your True North*, Chapter 11

Class XI case: Kent Thiry: Mayor of DaVita (HBS Case No. 410–065)

LDG: Discuss *The Discover Your True North Fieldbook*, Chapter 11

The purpose of this week's LDG is to solicit feedback from other members of the group about your leadership and your effectiveness in empowering other leaders.

Week XII: Global Leadership

Personal assignment: *The Discover Your True North Fieldbook*, Chapter 12

> Readings: *Discover Your True North*, Chapter 12 and Epilogue
>
> Class XII case: Unilever's Paul Polman: Developing Global Leaders (HBS Case No. 413–097)
>
> LDG: discuss *The Discover Your True North Fieldbook*, Chapter 12

Week XIII: Your Personal Leadership Development Plan (No class this week)

Personal assignment: *The Discover Your True North Fieldbook*, Chapter 13

> Readings:
>
> *Discover Your True North*, Afterword
>
> *Finding Your True North*, Epilogue
>
> (If your course permits time for a 13th class, it is recommended that you discuss:
>
> Case XIII: Alibaba Goes Public (HBS Case No. N9–115–029)
>
> LDG should focus on discussing each individual Personal Leadership Development Plan)

As the culmination of the course, complete your personal leadership development plan (PLDP) and turn it in. In doing so, you should refer back to and integrate all the previous exercises you have completed in the course.

Final Course Paper: The Purpose of My Leadership

In your final course paper, describe the purpose of your leadership and the principles and values that will guide your leadership. Discuss the areas of your authentic leadership development that you plan to focus on in the years ahead and the steps you will take to become an authentic leader.

About the Authors

Nick Craig is the president of the Authentic Leadership Institute (ALI), a leadership consulting firm teaching authentic leadership programs around the globe. ALI's mission is to help leaders and organizations discover their deeper purpose and have the courage to live it.

Nick's insights and approach come from more than 25 years working with top teams, senior leadership programs, executive coaching, and architecting results-focused change initiatives. Nick is the coauthor of "From Purpose to Impact" with Scott Snook in the May 2014 *Harvard Business Review*. His work in the area of authentic leadership and purpose has been used in corporate and academic settings, including GE, Unilever, and Wharton's Advanced Management Program. Nick's work as a Wharton fellow is documented at Wharton@Work. His article "Confidence is an Inside Job" is one of the most requested articles.

Beyond his involvement with Bill George, Nick has worked with Michael Beer, director emeritus of Harvard Business School's Organizational Change practice, helping top teams have honest dialogues that drive strategic implementation. He has also worked with MIT's Sloan School to develop their Leadership Center and executive coaching program based on the distributed leadership model.

For additional insights into the work of Nick and the Authentic Leadership Institute, please refer to the HBS Case "Unilever's Paul Polman: Developing Global Leaders," May 2013.

He currently lives in Harvard, MA, with his wife, Jeanne, and their kids, who teach Nick every day on how to become a more authentic partner and parent.

You can stay connected with Nick at www.authleadership.com.

Bill George is a senior fellow at Harvard Business School where he has taught leadership since 2004. He is the author of four best-selling books: *Authentic Leadership*, *True North*, *Finding Your True North*, and *7 Lessons for Leading in Crisis*, and coauthor of *True North Groups* with Doug Baker. He is faculty chair of HBS's executive education program Authentic Leadership Development and cochair of Leading Global Enterprises.

He was chief executive of Medtronic, the world's leading medical technology company, from 1991–2001. Under his leadership, Medtronic's market capitalization grew from $1.1 billion to $60 billion, averaging 35 percent a year. He currently serves as a director of Goldman Sachs and the Mayo Clinic, and recently served on the boards of ExxonMobil, Novartis, and Target.

He is the recipient of the 2014 Bower Award for Business Leadership from the Franklin Institute and was elected to the National Academy of Engineering in 2012. He has been named one of "Top 25 Business Leaders of the Past 25 Years" by PBS; "Executive of the Year" by the Academy of Management; and "Director of the Year" by the National Association of Corporate Directors.

He received his BSIE with high honors from Georgia Tech and his MBA with high distinction from Harvard University, where he was a Baker Scholar. During 2002, he was professor at IMD International and École Polytechnique in Lausanne, Switzerland, and executive-in-residence at Yale School of Management in 2003.

He and his wife, Penny, reside in Minneapolis, MN.

You can stay connected with Bill at www.billgeorge.org.

Scott Snook is a Senior Lecturer of Business Administration at the Harvard Business School where he teaches courses in leadership and leader development. He graduated with honors from West Point and was commissioned in the U.S. Army Corps of Engineers where he served in various command and staff positions for over 22 years, earning the rank of colonel before retiring in 2002. He has led soldiers in combat. Among his military decorations are the Legion of Merit, Bronze Star, Purple Heart, and Master Parachutist badge.

He has an MBA from Harvard Business School, where he graduated with high distinction as a Baker Scholar. Scott earned his PhD in organizational behavior from Harvard University, winning the Sage-Louis Pondy Best Dissertation Award from the Academy of Management for his study of the Friendly Fire Shoot-Down in Northern Iraq.

Until July 2002, Scott served as an academy professor in the Behavioral Sciences and Leadership Department at the U.S. Military Academy. He also directed West Point's Center for Leadership and Organizations Research as well as its joint master's program in leader development.

His book *Friendly Fire* received the 2002 Terry Award from the Academy of Management. Among his numerous publications, he coauthored a book that explores the role of common sense in leadership titled *Practical Intelligence in Everyday Life*, (2000), coedited *The Handbook for Teaching Leadership: Knowing, Doing, and Being* (2011), and coauthored the article "From Purpose to Impact" with Nick Craig in the May 2014 *Harvard Business Review*.

Scott has shared his leadership insights in formal executive education programs at Harvard and with numerous corporate audiences around the world.

Scott's research and consulting activities include leadership, leader development, leading change, organizational systems, and culture. He currently lives in Concord, MA, with his wife, Kathleen, and their five children.

You can stay connected with Scott at www.hbs.edu/faculty/Pages/profile.aspx?facId=164841.

ARE YOU AN AUTHENTIC LEADER?

To be a great leader and set your organization up for success, you must know yourself. Why? Find out in this instant classic, updated and expanded for today's professionals. In *Discover Your True North*, four-time bestselling author and Harvard Business School Professor Bill George guides you on a journey toward authenticity. On the way, he profiles 101 top business success stories from around the world, including Unilever's Paul Polman, PepsiCo's Indra Nooyi, Merck's Ken Frazier, Alibaba's Jack Ma, and The Huffington Post's Arianna Huffington. They've found their True North... and so can you.

"*Discover Your True North* is the most robust and practical leadership book I have ever read, period."

—TOM RATH, BESTSELLING AUTHOR OF
STRENGTHS FINDER 2.0 AND ARE YOU FULLY CHARGED?

"*Discover Your True North* bids to be a classic, standing alongside *The Effective Executive* by Peter Drucker and *Becoming a Leader* by Warren Bennis. I salute Bill on his best book."

– FOREWORD BY DAVID GERGEN